Introduction

To The Student

The purpose of this book is to ease you gently into the demands of Close Reading at Higher English. The exam you will sit in May (and probably in a Prelim) contains an extremely demanding test of Close Reading, with 50 marks' worth of questions testing your understanding of key ideas and your ability to analyse aspects of language and style.

For many students, at the beginning of their Higher English course, being plunged into full-scale Close Reading papers can be an alarming experience, since the combination of a complex passage and a series of over 20 very precise questions makes the task seem almost overwhelming.

The passages in this book are, in terms of length, topic, style and level of difficulty, very similar to those you will eventually see in exam papers (and NAB assessments). Working with them should make you familiar and, over time, more confident with writing of this type. The questions, however, are very different: instead of a large number of very detailed and technical questions, you will be faced here with just a small number (typically around five, but in one case just two) and nearly all of these will be multiple-choice – so all you have to do is read, think, and then write a single letter. In this way (unless you're foolish enough to make a series of wild guesses) you will concentrate on reading and not, at this stage, about worrying how to answer questions.

A word of warning, however: even though they are multiple-choice questions, there often isn't a "correct" answer (English is never really like that) and there will be much more value in your defending your choice by referring to the text and arguing your case than by simply giving yourself a tick or a cross.

An ever bigger word of warning: don't get too comfortable with the multiple-choice questions you'll see here, as they are never a feature of formal testing and assessment at Higher, and all too soon you will be having to come up with your own answers. If, however, you have worked sensibly through some or all of the material in this book, you will not be intimidated by the complexity of ideas and language you encounter in tests and exam papers and you will be a little more confident in dealing with some of the areas that are so often questioned in them.

With luck, you will find the passages here interesting and, in some cases, provocative enough to make you think about the topic and to question your own ideas. In test papers there isn't, it has to be admitted, much opportunity for genuine reflection on the topics, even though they are often of interest and importance. Discussion of the ideas in the passages with your teacher and your fellow students will be of real value; it should enable you to extend your understanding of some complex social issues and might even encourage you to explore some of the topics in more depth and possibly make use of this in your Writing assessment.

No one could sensibly claim that Close Reading at this level is "fun", but I hope that the material in this book makes it just a little bit less daunting for you than it might otherwise be.

To The Teacher or Lecturer

It is a truth universally acknowledged that the transition from Standard Grade or from Intermediate 2 to Higher is a difficult one, with students being launched into something much more challenging and having to come to terms with it very rapidly. This is especially true of Close Reading at Higher English, because the complexity of thought (and even just vocabulary) in the passages is markedly more demanding than both Credit and Intermediate 2.

There is an oft-repeated complaint that many students attempting Higher English are seriously unfamiliar with the type and style of writing in the passages on which they are questioned in the final Close Reading exam – it has been said, perhaps with some justification, that many encounter it only in past papers and on the day of the exam itself. They are almost intimidated by it, as if it is something from an alien world. Little wonder that so many find the whole business so challenging. Thus there is a pressing need for them to be exposed to this type of material as much as possible, simply in order to become more comfortable and more confident with it. That is what this book aims to do.

However, early exposure to the type of material **and** to the demanding types of question typical of the final examination is surely not a good way to achieve this de-mystification – indeed it is almost certainly counter-productive – yet all too often that is exactly what happens, because available materials are so exam-focused.

This book, therefore, is aimed at that stage when students are making the transition to Higher – be it in August of S5 or June of S4 or even earlier in S4. It contains 20 passages, all of which are similar in subject matter, level of difficulty, style, etc. to a typical exam (or NAB) passage. The passages have been drawn mostly from quality current journalism (as is the case with exam passages), but there are some book extracts as well. Many of the writers are ones whose work has featured in exams and other assessments (Ben Macintyre, Joyce McMillan, George Monbiot, Melanie Reid, Natasha Walter).

In this book, however, the passages are followed not by the usual gruelling set of questions, but by a short series of questions, mostly/exclusively multiple-choice or short response type, dealing mainly with overall understanding and key ideas, but touching also on some of the more common areas of "Analysis". In this way the pupils will concentrate, in this transitional stage, on **the process of reading and not on the process of answering questions**.

They will become, it is to be hoped, more comfortable with the type of writing, so that, when the closely-focused questions associated with formal testing are gradually introduced as the course progresses, students are able to focus more confidently on handling these, having to an extent overcome their "fear" of the passages themselves.

In addition, sensible use of the material in this book should:

- demonstrate by example such key matters as line of thought, use of evidence, structure, and tone – to the benefit not just of students' Close Reading skills but of their own writing (e.g. in internal assessment of Writing and of Personal Study as well as for the Critical Essay in the examination)

- suggest topics or open up ideas which students might go on to explore in their own Writing work

- inform students generally about important issues of the day or about interesting topics which might otherwise escape their attention

- in some of the passages, challenge conventional thinking and allow genuine reflection on the subject matter without being diverted into working through an exhaustive series of questions

- be a useful preparation for the "comparison questions", which require an overview of passages, something not easily sustained while answering all the detailed questions

- encourage an interest in reading such material "at source" in quality journalism or suitable works of non-fiction.

A note on the use of multiple-choice questions

The decision to use multiple-choice questions was not taken lightly. Their effectiveness in meaningful formal assessment of any English skills that matter is very limited. This book, however, is not about formal testing – it is about introducing students to the complex ideas and language features typical of those they will encounter, later, in Close Reading assessments. The questions, therefore, should be seen not as "tests" but as triggers for thought and discussion.

As every English teacher knows, multiple-choice questions in English are either ridiculously simple ("This passage is about: A – Mountaineering; B – Nuclear Physics; C – Hairdressing") or so subtly nuanced that no one can agree on the right answer ("The word 'enervated' means: A – run down; B – very tired; C – drained"). The questions in this book tend to the latter, and it is quite likely that teachers (and students) will not agree with the "answers". That doesn't really matter. What will matter, of course, is the discussion about the disagreement.

It must be stressed to the students, of course, and stressed very forcefully, that there will, in their "proper" Close Reading assessments, be no place whatsoever for multiple-choice questions.

Some final points about using this book

The passages are presented in (a very approximate) order of difficulty, but it is not necessary to work through them strictly in order.

At least one question on each passage touches on "Analysis", but there has been no attempt to organise these in a systematic way such that it will "teach" the skills required to tackle this type of question. Each passage throws up its own unique features of style, and students must get used to the idea that each example of imagery or sentence structure must be analysed in the context in which it appears and that there is never an off-the-shelf answer. (For a detailed and structured approach to learning about all the key areas of Analysis, teachers and students should refer to Part One of "Scottish Examination Materials: Higher English Close Reading" (9780340928080, 2007) published by Hodder Gibson, to which this book is in many respects an introduction.)

A variety of ways to use this book could be employed:

- traditional reading in class, followed by question-answering and discussion

- "pressure" reading and question-answering in a limited time

- group activities to reach "consensus" answers (to be defended against other groups)

- reading and question-answering as homework, followed by discussion in class time.

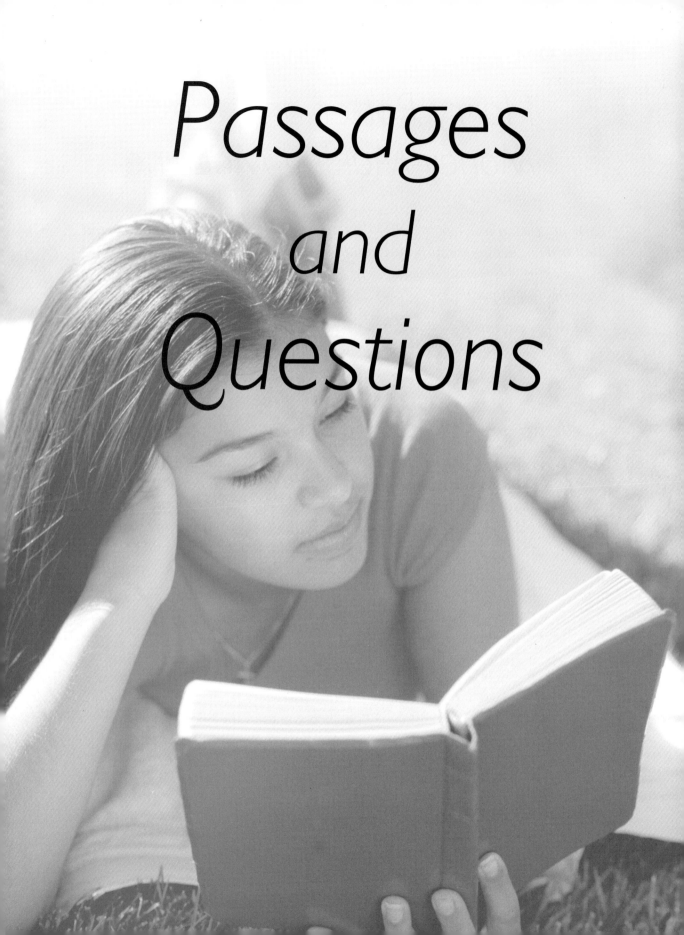

Passages
and
Questions

Harry Potter and the Money-Making Machine

Early in 2007, it was reported that J K Rowling had completed the seventh and final book in her enormously successful Harry Potter series. In this article, published in The Herald *newspaper in February 2007, Melanie Reid is glad that the series is at an end.*

Read the passage straight through to get an overall impression of her reasons for not liking the whole "Harry Potter phenomenon". Then answer the questions that follow.

1   There are some things which have to be said, even if they make one desperately unpopular with a nation's children. Some of us - and I'm speaking in a whisper here - are glad that the seventh and final Harry Potter book has been finished. In fact, not to put too fine a
5   point on it, some of us are indescribably, heel-clickingly overjoyed that J K Rowling has written "The End" for the last time. Some of us - well, OK, quite a lot of us - have come to regard Harry the global brand as a total bore, as predictable as Coca-Cola, as stimulating as a Big Mac and as profitable as Nike. We will be happy never to hear
10   the name mentioned again.

It is not exaggerating to describe the way in which Harry has dominated popular taste for the past decade or so as cultural tyranny. An astonishing 325 million copies of the books have been sold around the world, which has little to do with the merits of a
15   jolly saga about a boy wizard battling evil, but everything to do with the power of the marketing industry, with children who are both less literate and more overtly consumer-conscious than previous generations, and with parents clutching at a liferaft in the sea of their busy lives.

20 The Harry Potter books are, as entertainment, inoffensive. But they're not literature; they're middle-brow pot-boilers. I will not go as far as Professor Harold Bloom of Yale University, who has said of J K Rowling's work: "The writing was dreadful; the book was terrible. Rowling's mind is so governed by clichés and dead
25 metaphors that she has no other style of writing."

But I'm with Bloom in his demolition of the well-rehearsed argument which says that at least children are reading something, and that Harry Potter will lead them on to a life of reading – and, by inference, erudition. Now the first part of this argument does have
30 something going for it: no doubt some children who would otherwise have spent their lives playing "Grand Theft Auto: Vice City" on their games console have been rescued from zombiedom by the gripping tales of Voldemort and Hogwarts.

➢

But the second part doesn't hold water. Harry Potter will not lead
35   children on to *Swallows and Amazons*, the *Just So* Stories, *Wind
in the Willows* or *Alice through The Looking Glass*. What it will
do, as Professor Bloom declared, is train them to read Stephen King.

Certainly, in my own experience, the craze for Harry Potter books
was a peer group thing for children, not unrelated to wearing the
40   right brand of trainers. They were bought as status symbols and then
languished, a quarter read, for years under the bed. How many of
those 325 million copies failed to change the trajectory of the
modern TV-raised child who, tragically, does not read for pleasure
and probably never will? More than a few, I suspect.

45   So that's the elitist argument against Rowling, if you like: that her
work is part of a general dumbing down; that in a way the whole
Potter phenomenon represents a missed opportunity to stretch
children's imaginations and teach millions the use of supple,
challenging, original writing.

50   Maybe it's all a little harsh. Rowling's books are not that bad and
have brought pleasure to millions. I remember as a child exactly the
same kind of literary snobbery attaching to Enid Blyton books.
Where I really quarrel with Harry Potter, however, is not in the
quality of the writing but in the marketing. This Harry – Harry the
55   brand – really is a monster of the first order. Somewhere along the
line the author waved bye bye to her creation and saw it become a
global money-making colossus, one which exploited the thrill of the
chase and the tribal yearning to be part of something. It wasn't a
book; it was a badge of belonging, a cult.

60   Oh, we fell for it. We were sent to spend nights queuing in the cold
on Sauchiehall Street, in order to be the first to purchase one of
those doorstopper hardbacks to review for our employers. This is
when I perceived another worrying phenomenon: the rise of the
adult fan. Frequently, the grown-ups queuing for their copy weren't

➤

65 doing it for nieces or nephews, but for themselves. In some cases their lips were moving when they scanned the lines, in other cases they didn't even have that excuse.

Far more worrying are the adults who have latched on to Harry Potter. One adult female Potter fan in the States emailed a colleague
70 of mine, who had written an article about Rowling's penning of the final sentence, telling him she felt an "emotional, intellectual and personal" connection with him because of what he had written. The books, she said, had made her reflect on her own childhood and she was "enriched and satisfied".

75 Now all this is very sweet; and one can only be pleased that she and millions of fans like her are happy, but one does have to question whether J K Rowling is now being hijacked into territories which she never intended to visit. In that sense it is interesting that both the author and the young actor, Daniel Radcliffe, who plays Harry in
80 the (largely lamentable) films, have expressed sincere relief at the end of the saga. Is it too presumptuous to suggest that everyone creative connected with Harry has been imprisoned for too long in an immense money-making machine; one which has come close to crushing the original joy of an adequate story?

Questions

1   Which **two** of the following are the main reasons for the writer's disapproval of the Harry Potter books?

    A   The quality of writing is poor.

    B   The whole thing grew into an enormous commercial enterprise.

    C   Too many adults were reading the books.

    D   Children owned the books but often did not read them.

    E   Children wanted them for the wrong reasons.

    F   They are not actually very good entertainment.

2   Which **one** of the following statements is true?

    A   The writer agrees with Professor Bloom about the quality of writing in the books.

    B   The writer disagrees with Professor Bloom about the quality of writing in the books.

    C   The writer agrees with Professor Bloom that reading the books will not develop children's love of good literature.

    D   The writer disagrees with Professor Bloom that reading the books will not develop children's love of good literature.

3 (a)   Here are five quotations from the passage which make quite positive, complimentary comments about the books and their influence. Rank them in order from "most complimentary" to "least complimentary".

    A   "the merits of a jolly saga" (lines 14–15)

    B   "the Harry Potter books are, as entertainment, inoffensive" (line 20)

    C   "some children … have been rescued from zombiedom" (lines 30–32)

    D   "not that bad" (line 50)

    E   "have brought pleasure to millions" (line 51)

Questions

(b) Here are six quotations from the passage which make quite critical, slightly offensive comments about the books and their influence. Rank them in order from "most offensive" to "least offensive".

A "a total bore" (line 8)

B "cultural tyranny" (lines 12–13)

C "middle-brow pot-boilers" (line 21)

D "part of a general dumbing down" (line 46)

E "really is a monster of the first order" (line 55)

F "a global money-making colossus" (lines 56–57)

4 Consider carefully the title given to this passage: "Harry Potter and the Money-Making Machine". Which **two** of the following features of the title are most effective in suggesting the writer's critical attitude in the passage as a whole?

(i) the use of alliteration in "Money-Making Machine"

(ii) linking the character's name with money

(iii) the use of "machine" to suggest something inhuman

(iv) making it sound like a typical "Harry Potter" title

A (i) and (ii)

B (ii) and (iii)

C (iii) and (iv)

D (i) and (iv)

E (ii) and (iv)

Change our Schools, Not our Children

In this passage, Johann Hari, writing in The Independent *newspaper in March 2007, questions the way we treat children who have "Attention Deficit Hyperactivity Disorder", known as ADHD.*

Read the passage straight through to get a general grasp of why Hari feels treatment with drugs such as Ritalin is not a good idea. Then answer the questions that follow.

1   One of my cousins – a manic, smart six-year-old who finds sit-down-and-shut-up school excruciating – was diagnosed a year ago with Attention Deficit Hyperactivity Disorder (ADHD). He now quietly pops Ritalin, a drug that is chemically almost identical to cocaine,
5   and sits more passively on the settee, at the desk or in the car, concentrating on whatever is put in front of him. He's not alone: the number of children taking the drug has surged by an average of 31 per cent every year since 1999.

So I was intrigued when I heard that Dr Robert Spitzer, the
10 psychiatrist who first identified ADHD and introduced it to the medical journals, now believes up to a third of such diagnoses are "mistaken". Another expert says many of these kids are being drugged simply for "displaying normal reactions which are not really disorders at all".

15 This is bad enough – but the more I burrowed into the ADHD literature, the more I began to believe that the problems with ADHD in our kids point to wider problems in our Attention Deficit Democracy, and especially in the way we teach our children.

➤

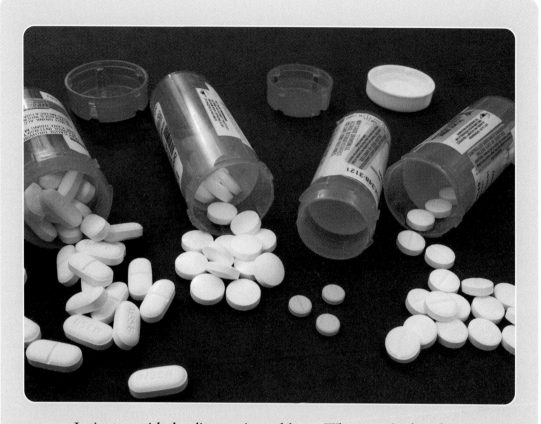

Let's start with the diagnostic problems. When you look at the criteria
20 for classifying a child with ADHD – quickly bored, abandons projects
that don't interest him, restlessness – they are easily mistaken for the
qualities shown by a clever child. Indeed, one of the questions asked
in the initial identification of ADHD is "Does your child 'act smart'?"
A significant number of the misdiagnosed cases may well be children
25 who are persistently rebelling against a regimented and tedious
school system and end up being drugged for it.

Our schools are still overwhelmingly based on the outdated model
of a factory, preparing kids to sit in rows, be obedient and get ready
for five working decades of the same. It was always barbaric, but
30 now – with our economy requiring more creativity and
entrepreneurship from more of the population – it's also bad
economics. Does anybody think that drilling children in groups of
30 to be prepared for dull and repetitive tests is the best way to
create a questioning, thinking populace?

➢

35 It is no coincidence that ADHD and Ritalin have risen as corporal punishment was phased out. Until the 1970s, the dull factory model of schooling was upheld with the sanction of physical force: if you didn't sit through it obediently, you were beaten. Now that is (thankfully) no longer permitted, we have replaced the cane with a cane-for-the-brain.

40 But the problem does not lie solely in misdiagnosing ADHD – it's also in how we understand it, and what we do with the "sufferers". The most prominent way of understanding ADHD today is the "biomedical model", which sees it as an objective neurological problem, arising from genetic abnormalities in the brain. The 45 followers of this model point to brain scans which show that people with ADHD have differently constituted brains. But London taxi drivers have a larger hippocampus than the rest of us, because they are constantly exercising this mental muscle to find streets. Similarly, people with ADHD might have a different-shaped brain 50 because of the way they behave, rather than the other way round.

There is another, better way of understanding ADHD: "the farmer-hunter hypothesis". Some 10,000 years ago, humans moved from being hunter-societies, where impulsiveness, restlessness and risk-taking were essential for survival, to being farmer-societies, where it 55 was more important to be predictable, dependable and obedient. Kids with ADHD have all the impulses of a hunter society, yet they are stuck in a settled farmers' world.

This theory chimed instinctively with the experience of my cousin. When I see him dying to jump up and run around, it strikes me how 60 unnatural it is to expect a six-year-old boy to want to be cooped up all day, sitting in a chair, and then come home and do homework. He seems to be almost physically twitching to run through fields and spear animals.

But given that we aren't going to return to the (actually pretty 65 miserable) life of pre-modern hunters, are ADHD people just an

➤

evolutionary dead end? On the contrary – many of these skills are extremely useful now. A number of entrepreneurs and artists exhibit the symptoms: for example, David Neeleman, founder of JetBlue Airways and inventor of the e-ticket, says his success is "entirely
70 due" to ADHD. Thinking about a dozen things at once, hating being told what to do – these might make you a nightmare pupil, but they often make you a successful grown-up.

The "farmer-hunter" theory is valuable because it shows that ADHD "sufferers" have different, but not inferior brains. Following this
75 theory, a successful school has been set up in the States, in New Hampshire, for children with ADHD, which, rather than drugging them so they can sit through the tedium of the chalk-and-talk schooling revered by the educational establishment, keeps them as stimulated as their brains require. Our government should be prescribing less Ritalin
80 and building more schools like this, instead of becoming more conservative, and reverting to disengaged, just-listen classes.

There's an interesting historical analogy for the decision to medicalise children's natural resistance to this. In 1851, a Louisiana physician called Samuel L Cartwright identified an "illness" he called
85 "drapetomania" (drapeto comes from a Greek word meaning "to run away"), which afflicted runaway slaves, compelling them to escape. "With proper medical treatment, strictly followed, this troublesome practice that many negroes have of running away can be entirely prevented," he counselled. And with proper medical treatment, we
90 can make children accept an excruciating, test-obsessed model of schooling.

This isn't just bad for kids with ADHD – and the tens of thousands who have been misdiagnosed with it – but it's bad for a country that needs engaged, thinking adults. For more than a decade now, we
95 have been chemically altering huge numbers of our children to fit into this flat, failing model of education. Wouldn't it be better to change the education system to fit our children?

Questions

1 Which one of the following statements best sums up the writer's main objection to the use of drugs to treat ADHD?

    A He believes it damages the children who have ADHD.

    B He believes it is dangerous for those who don't actually have ADHD.

    C He believes ADHD should be treated by more appropriate schools not by drugs.

    D He believes ADHD is not a condition which requires medical treatment at all.

    E He believes it is like punishing children who have ADHD.

2 Which one of the following statements best describes the writer's main criticism of schools today?

    A They demand passivity and conformity.

    B They have abolished corporal punishment.

    C They do not train teachers to cope with problem children.

    D They are out of date.

    E They are geared to the passing of exams.

3 (a) Which one of the following best describes the writer's purpose in introducing and describing the "hunter-farmer hypothesis" (lines 51–63)?

    A to justify his claim that ADHD should not be treated as a disorder

    B to explain why some children are very reckless and unsettled

    C to demonstrate the difference between two different types of personality

    D to help explain how well he now understands his cousin

    E to explain the success of David Neeleman

  (b) Which one of the following best describes the writer's purpose in introducing the "historical analogy" he refers to in lines 81–91?

    A to show the dangers of treating ADHD as a medical condition

    B to show the stupidity of treating ADHD as a medical condition

    C to show the difficulties of treating ADHD as a medical condition

    D to show the absurdity of treating ADHD as a medical condition

    E to show the advantages of treating ADHD as a medical condition

Questions

4 (a) Here are six quotations from the passage in which the writer conveys his very critical opinion of today's schools. Rank them in order from "most critical" to "least critical".

A "sit-down-and-shut-up school" (lines 1–2)

B "barbaric" (line 29)

C "dull and repetitive tests" (line 33)

D "tedium of the chalk-and-talk schooling" (line 77)

E "disengaged, just-listen classes" (line 81)

F "flat, failing model of education" (line 96)

(b) The writer ends the passage with a rhetorical question – to which he clearly expects the answer "yes". What **tone** do you think he is trying to adopt?

A pleading

B reasonable

C aggressive

D angry

E persuasive

F pessimistic

Tipping the Scales

This passage, written by Polly Toynbee, discusses some of the causes of obesity in Britain and how it might be reduced. It was written for The Guardian, *a newspaper which is commonly regarded as having a "middle class" readership.*

Read the passage straight through in order to get a grasp of her key argument. Then answer the questions that follow.

1   This obesity debate is full of humbug and denial. Fat is a class issue, but few like to admit that most of the seriously obese are poor. This is not about the nanny state telling toffs to keep off the claret in their clubs. It's about people like us telling people down there in the
5   underclass to eat up their greens. Health professionals say "we" must take more exercise and stop eating fast food, but mostly they really mean "them".

True, many of us middle classes are overweight, but most of the dangerously obese – the 22% with a body-mass index in the red zone
10   – are to be found carless on council estates and not in the leafy suburbs where kids are driven to school in supertanker 4x4s. It is poor children at most risk of swelling up like balloons, in danger of losing limbs and eyesight to diabetes as they grow up. It's wrong to talk about "fat cats" when the privileged are usually thin and sleek
15   with bodies well-exercised by gyms and personal trainers on diets of radicchio and sparkling water.

Some experts, reluctant to appear over-critical, look for sympathetic reasons why the poor are fat and unhealthy. Fresh fruit and vegetables are so expensive, they say. There is no transport to get
20   from estates to the good food shops. Poor women are too hard-pressed to have time to cook proper family meals, so they snack. It's

➤

hard for poor children to exercise in dangerous concrete jungles, with no cars to take them to ballet and judo lessons. Or maybe, sadly, these people just don't know what's good for them.

25 All these may be contributory factors. The uneducated may not read small print on deliberately incomprehensible food labels to detect the difference between kJ and kcal. Unlike neurotic middle-class mothers, they may not follow every scare about tartrazine and GM or dream up hypochondriacal allergies for lack of anything else to
30 worry about in what is, remember, the safest and healthiest time ever.

So why are the poor getting dangerously fat? They are, mainly, a little better off and food has got cheaper. They are not ignorant. Every woman alive has spent her life obsessing over body size,

➢

35   perusing every diet in magazines and daytime TV shows. Never has
      there been more information about what food is fattening and what
      is not. Public health advice is puny beside this great surfeit of diet
      and fitness info.

      What's more, these messages are vigorously reinforced by every
40   fashion and celeb page telling us thin is beautiful, fat is horrible.
      Tabloids spend fortunes on paparazzi snaps of some celeb on the
      beach who has "let herself go". Star-cellulite-in-bikini is worth as
      much as star-in-illicit-love-nest. No child needs to be told fat is bad
      when right from nursery school it's the fat kids that get tormented
45   for being slow, ugly and undesirable – often reinforced by teachers
      who see them as losers, too. From Charlie and the Chocolate Factory
      to Harry Potter, heroes are skinny and lithe, while nasty children are
      fat porkers.

      So what's gone wrong? Most of us wrestle with food, torn between
50   denial and desire, between fridge and gym, eating and regretting. It
      is very hard and girth grows by the decade. Most people I know live
      in an endless cycle of boom and bust with the weighing scales. But
      mostly the middle class stays the right side of dangerously obese. In
      the highest echelons, those superthin lettuce-eaters know that
55   thinness radiates high status. "You can't be too rich or too thin," said
      Dorothy Parker.

      Fat means poor and out of control. People who feel they have no
      control over their own lives give up. What's there to struggle and
      make sacrifices for? No job, no prospects, no point. A little of what
60   you fancy compensates for life's big disappointments. So drinking
      and smoking and eating the wrong things become small treats in
      desolate lives. Being out of control becomes a mindset ever harder
      to climb out of. No job becomes no status, no hope and, rapidly,
      unemployable semi-despair, whatever the job market out there.

65   Poor children at school know their low status from the day they

walk in. The little girl with perfect kit, sparkly trainers and lovely lunchbox is always admired over the shabby kid who never went to ballet and only had a packet of Wotsits for breakfast. The rest of us have very good social incentives not to give in to temptation – and
70 even then often fail – but those who have nothing easily give up.

The traditional middle-class reaction is to teach poor mothers how to become better managers; a family can eat healthily on very little, they opine. See how low-paid vicars bring up their broods on a pittance. Though when I recently tried living on the minimum wage,
75 even without children, I found I couldn't manage, counting every penny and eating nothing but lentils, rice, potatoes, pasta, cabbage and oranges. It's a miserable, life-denying way to eat, but that's not the point. Even with more money, the poor would probably eat themselves into an early grave if there was not much else to live for.
80 Why defer gratification if there isn't going to be any compensating gratification?

It is inequality and disrespect that makes people fat: obesity took off 25 years ago, up 400% in the years when inequality has exploded. People will only get thinner when they are included in things that
85 are worth staying thin for. Offer self-esteem, respect, jobs or some social status and the pounds would start to fall away.

Of course, we need tough labelling laws and a ban on advertising junk to children in schools and on TV. Of course it's a disgrace that there are virtually no safe cycle lanes in cities. Of course every
90 school needs great dance, aerobics, sport and fun in after-school clubs. But let's not fool ourselves: only a genuine drive towards a society that doesn't leave out a quarter of its citizens will send the bathroom scales tipping in the right direction.

Questions

1 "Most of the seriously obese are poor" (line 2)

What according to the writer in the passage as a whole is the main reason for this?

A Poor people have an unhealthy diet.

B Poor people cannot afford healthy food.

C Poor people are unable to exercise properly.

D Poor people don't understand food-labelling.

E Poor people lack status in society.

2 Re-read lines 32–48.

Why does the writer go into so much detail to demonstrate that "thin is beautiful, fat is horrible" (line 40)? Choose one of the following:

A to show how pervasive this impression is in the media

B to express her incredulity that so many people are fat

C to point out there can't be a simple reason for obesity among the poor

D to remind us that everyone knows they should avoid unhealthy eating

E to suggest that our acceptance of this is a serious part of the problem

3 Why, according to the writer, are "low paid vicars" able to "bring up their broods on a pittance"?

A They have a purpose in life.

B They know how to buy healthy food cheaply.

C They know how to handle money.

D They tend not to smoke or drink.

E They understand about nutrition.

4 In lines 17–24, the writer is fairly scornful about the "experts" she describes. Which one of the following most effectively conveys this tone?

A "so expensive, they say"

B "the good food shops"

C "dangerous concrete jungles"

D "ballet and judo lessons"

E "just don't know what's good for them"

Questions

5   In the last paragraph (lines 87–93) the writer concludes with a strong and passionate summary of her main argument.

Here is a list of some language features she employs in this paragraph to add power to her writing. Rank them in order of how important you think each is in achieving this. (Start with "most important".)

A   the repetition of "Of course"

B   the strong word choice such as "tough", "junk" and "disgrace"

C   the listing of the desirable activities in schools

D   the use of "But" after the third "Of course"

E   the use of a colon to introduce the final point

Desperate Dan

In September 2004 the publishers of the comic called The Dandy *announced
that one of its longest-running characters, Desperate Dan, was being "updated".
In this passage, which appeared in* The Times *newspaper, writer and columnist
Ben Macintyre gives his reaction to this news and explores the way characters
in comics have had to change over the years.*

*Read the passage straight through to get a general grasp of Macintyre's reaction
to the changes and why he thinks the original characters were so appealing.
Then answer the questions that follow.*

1 The plight of Desperate Dan just became a little more desperate. *The
Dandy*, the world's longest-running comic, is being updated, and
with it the familiar cartoon character with the bristling chin shaped
like a chest of drawers and the taste for cow pie. The muscular
5 cowboy is giving up his gun, and losing weight, and generally
cleaning up his act. Moreover, he is being joined by a new set of
"cool" characters deemed more relevant to modern children:
Dreadlock Holmes, an Afro-Caribbean streetwise boy detective, and
Jak, a schoolboy with a spiky haircut but "a sense of responsibility".

10 This may be further proof of the ineluctable march of political
correctness, but more than that, the imposition of "responsibility"
on comic characters strikes at the very heart of what has made *The
Dandy* and its later rivals so enjoyable to children (mostly boys, it is
true) for the past 67 years. Unlike Jak, Dennis the Menace in *The
15 Beano* is by definition irresponsible, a figure of unrepentant
anarchy; Beryl the Peril in *The Topper* is a threat, not a role model.
The idea that Dreadlock Holmes should be solving misdemeanours
rather than committing them is a sign of just how far comic heroes
have come from the original, enchanting ideal of misbehaviour.

➤

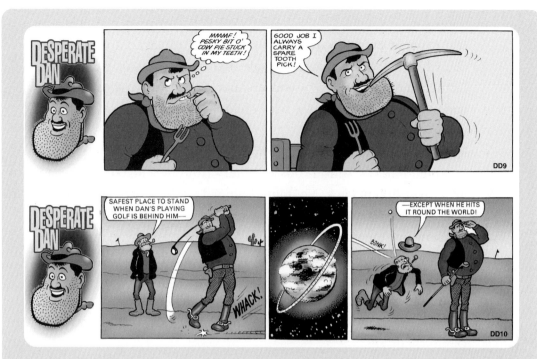

20 Comics, like every other form of children's entertainment, must now be morally loaded, packed with improving messages and role models, sanitised and uplifting.

A short biography of Desperate Dan illustrates the point. Born in 1937, shortly after the launch of *The Dandy*, Dan, an inhabitant of
25 Cactusville, Texas, was a thumping, gluttonous cowboy, whose unawareness of his own strength ensured rolling, permanent mayhem: he smashed things up, he devoured animals whole, he punched down trees without feeling a thing, he shaved with a blowtorch; he was quite wonderful, and an entire generation of
30 children adored him. He was a figure from myth, the giant with the mind of a child. In the 1950s, sales of *The Dandy* reached two million.

But then the world changed, and like cowboys before him, Dan found himself an anachronism. In the 1980s, the character known for inhaling entire bales of tobacco through a drainpipe was forced
35 to give up smoking. The horrors of "mad cow disease" in 1996 restricted Dan's traditional diet, and cow pie came off the menu for

fear it might be mad cow pie. There were furious complaints from animal lovers when Dan ate whale and chips. Fear of paedophilia further undermined Dan's image – no longer was it acceptable to
40 depict an adult hanging out with children.

In 1997, there was an attempt to do away with Dan completely, and he sailed into the sunset, but an outcry from nostalgic middle-aged men brought him back. No doubt Dan will continue to survive in the new, revamped comic, but the character is not what he was: the
45 formerly ballooning stomach has shifted upwards into an impressive barrel chest, as Dan has cut down on the calories; the cartoon violence has stopped; he has even hung up his spurs to avoid hurting his horse. Dan, says his editor, "has had his edges smoothed out". Yet without his edges, this is no longer Desperate Dan – it is
50 Diminished Dan.

Comics, like all media, move with the times. Lord Snooty of *The Beano* with his aristocratic Eton collar was done away with in 1990, a victim of class prejudice; Corporal Clott did not long survive the end of National Service; Little Plum, the Red Indian squaw who was
55 deemed a demeaning depiction of native American culture, vanished from *The Dandy* in 1994. The belt and the cane, dual threats that loomed over comic miscreants for decades, have gone, no longer permissible given modern attitudes to corporal punishment. Looking farther back, the girls' comics of the 1920s and 1930s seem
60 quaintly sexist, and the patriotic picture stories for boys in publications such as *Victor* and *Hotspur* positively weird in their jingoism.

As the first "literature" read by many children, comics undoubtedly play a role in shaping young minds. But there is a gulf of difference
65 between the grim racial stereotyping of certain comics in the early part of the past century, and seeking to turn Desperate Dan into a poster boy for peace and proper nutrition. The magic of *The Beano* and *The Dandy* in their heyday lay in the sheer naughtiness they

celebrated. The characters were cheeky and exuberant, always in
trouble with Teacher or Dad, persistently subversive and always
happily punished for it. Like William in the *Just William* stories,
Dennis the Menace and his faithful dog Gnasher were symbols of
childish insurrection, thrillingly wicked to anyone under ten. It is
surely no accident that these comics reached the peak of their
popularity in the 1950s, as Britain emerged from the years of war-
time austerity, strict rules and good behaviour. These comics made
unruliness and childhood fun.

In the modern world of Disney, children are constantly bombarded
and badgered with saccharine-coated stories of moral improvement.
The delight of the old comics was that they allowed children to
retreat, without being lectured, into a world composed entirely of
things that children love: general misbehaviour and jokes at the
expense of adults. Some of that cheekiness endures in the modern
versions of these comics, but by introducing characters with "an
awareness of social responsibility" much of the joyful anarchy will
surely be lost.

Comics are barometers of the culture, for better and worse.
Desperate Dan may now be on his best behaviour, in obedience to
modern standards of political correctness; yet the lantern-jawed
cowboy is a lone survivor from an earlier, less paranoid age, when a
cartoon character could eat cow pie without fear that young and
impressionable readers would immediately go out and imitate him,
by devouring a cow.

Questions

1 Which one of the following statements best sums up the writer's main point about the changes to "Desperate Dan"?

   A They are necessary in order to comply with modern attitudes.

   B They will make Dan less appealing to young readers.

   C They are a regrettable symptom of modern attitudes.

   D They will help steer young people away from bad habits.

   E They will refresh the cartoon and bring Dan up to date.

2 Which of the following words best describes the writer's attitude to the changes:

   A amused

   B angry

   C pleased

   D saddened

   E confused

3 Re-read lines 51–86. Clearly, Macintyre prefers the older versions of the comics to the modern ones. Which one of the following best explains why?

   A They were about children breaking rules.

   B They were sexist and racist.

   C They made breaking the rules seem fun.

   D They didn't tell readers how to behave.

   E They were an antidote to post-war austerity.

4 Explain briefly, without quoting directly from the passage, what the writer finds unacceptable about the two new characters being introduced to *The Dandy*.

   (a) Dreadlock Holmes

   (b) Jak

A Nation of TV Addicts

In September 2003 the Chief Inspector of Schools in England and Wales reported that many children were starting Primary school unable to talk or to carry out basic social tasks. In the passage which follows, from The Times *newspaper, writer and broadcaster Libby Purves thinks she has found the main cause of the problem.*

Read the passage straight through in order to get a general grasp of Purves' criticisms of TV, especially when watched by young children. Then answer the questions that follow.

1 It seems that increasing numbers of five-year-olds are arriving at school barely able to converse or behave – in fact less well-prepared for school than they have ever been before. Whereas 20 years ago there might be one or two "problem" children in each intake,
5 needing to be civilised by the school community, nowadays reception teachers expect that a substantial number of apparently normal five-year-olds will be unable to communicate, to sit still, to fasten their buttons or to use a knife and fork.

You can blame "broken" homes and "dysfunctional" families, but
10 they are a minority. You can tut about working mothers, but current housing and living costs mean that the average family needs 1.5 jobs to stay secure. But when we look at the particular qualities of these new problem children – not hostility or misbehaviour as much as social ineptness and inarticulacy – there is something we do not
15 blame enough: we are a nation of TV addicts, and infant lives are being degraded by it. There is an epidemic raging, and we barely notice.

One in three UK children under four years old has a private television in the bedroom. Even among those who don't, the use of

➤

20   TV as a babysitter is widespread. We are not talking here about brief interludes, when a meal is being prepared, for example; we are talking about children who – like 86 per cent of those surveyed – watch for up to six hours a day. Seven per cent watched even more.

  For tens of thousands of pre-school children, solitude with the TV is
25   the norm, rather than a treat. Either they get it at home, with parents too busy, self-absorbed, depressed, drugged or emotionally chaotic to care what happens as long as the child causes no noise or mess; or else they are in the home of a relative or poor-quality childminder who never turns it off. Even some nurseries have a screen flickering
30   all day. There are homes – many of them middle-class, clean and tidy – where the TV goes on at dawn and is never off. There are children who have hardly ever had a one-to-one conversation, and who are lulled to sleep by bedroom videos and dvds. There are plenty of small children who are well-fed, own toys and even get the

occasional bedtime story, but they still spend far, far too long with the screen.

In homes without gardens or space, in an age when the simple domestic tasks of yesterday are over more quickly (and the safety culture means we are afraid to share them with children anyway in case they cut or burn themselves) we have let the television fill the vacuum. Certainly, nobody has had the bottle to offer new parents a TV health warning, as government does about carbon monoxide or passive smoking.

This matters. It really does. Television is a mild hypnotic: studies measuring brain activity find that even when viewers are apparently mentally involved, after a few minutes the oscillation between alpha and beta brain waves ceases, in favour of a flat, spaced out, alpha/alpha pattern. We all know the effect. At the end of a long day's work we rather treasure it. But it is not a suitable way for a developing infant to spend its day.

A small child is a miracle: programmed to ardent curiosity, exploration and laying down a vital understanding of the basics concerning the physical universe, communication and the nature of other people and animals. The longer a child spends watching television in these formative, plastic, impressionable first years the less chance it has to develop any such understanding. And that applies even to the most child-friendly videos and thoughtful channels such as CBeebies. Even without exposure to violence and sexuality, even assuming a censoring, "careful" home, there is damage.

TV has its merits, but it does not respond. It does not correct your mistaken impressions, it does not hug you, or move around the room, clown in response to your clowning or lead you to the window to look at a rainbow or a pigeon. All it does is follow its own agenda, grinding mechanically through its tricks without any

➢

reference to your personality or your response. It does not know you are there. Yet it is, with its flickering and its colour, hypnotically fascinating: it physically holds your attention for longer than you really want to bestow it.

70 Those too young to understand its limitations should have it rationed, by adults. TV for an under-five should be one of many activities in the day, shared and discussed. A child watching a programme with an adult or an older sibling is having a fairly social, instructive experience. A child alone with a screen is not. Yet,
75 because small children hunger and thirst after knowledge, that child will be concentrating, taking cues from what it sees and irrationally hoping for a response. The response will not come: after a while, the child stops hoping. The screen may be a poor babysitter, but it is an influential one. It teaches you that life is a spectator sport, and
80 that you as an individual don't matter. This is not a good start.

Adults, even teenagers, are welcome to slump in front of the telly and go to hell in a handcart if they want. We are fully formed people; we can make the return journey from that passive limbo. But under-fives are more vulnerable. If, in those first few years, a
85 child can't lay down a basic template of social interaction, spoken communication and playful partnership, it is a lasting handicap. We shouldn't tolerate it, any more than we would tolerate sending them up chimneys. Indeed, neurologically and socially it was probably better to be a slum child playing in a grubby gutter with a soap-box
90 cart and a roughneck sibling, than to be a well-fed, clean-clothed, dull-eyed TV slave six hours a day. A child in a carpet factory in the Third World is learning more effectively than a Western toddler alone for hours with a screen.

Questions

1 Which one of the following statements best sums up the writer's main reason for believing that TV is bad for young children?

    A It leads to TV addiction in later life.

    B It is used as a substitute babysitter.

    C It discourages them from physical activity.

    D It hinders the development of their brains.

    E It means they have little conversation with parents.

2 In line 30 the writer adds the parenthetical comment "– many of them middle-class, clean and tidy –". Which of the following do you think is her main reason for doing so:

    A because you might expect better of middle-class homes

    B as a criticism of these middle-class homes

    C to avoid appearing snobbish

    D to show how widespread the problem is

    E to emphasise that the middle classes are guilty as well

3 Re-read lines 61–69. In this paragraph the writer uses a number of techniques to emphasise her criticism of TV. Which one of theses do you think is the most effective in the paragraph?

    A word choice, such as "hypnotically" and "rainbow"

    B personification in "hug", "move"

    C listing in the second sentence

    D repetition of "it does not ..."

    E imagery in "grinding ..."

4 The paragraph in lines 70–80 contains nine sentences. Using your knowledge of the writer's point of view in the passage as a whole, decide which **one** of these sentences you think is the most important.

Questions

5 Look again at the very last sentence of the passage. Which **two** of the following do you think best describes the effect the writer's purpose in concluding the passage in this way.

(i) to be informative

(ii) to sum up her argument

(iii) to shock

(iv) to upset

(v) to be provocative

(vi) to exaggerate

A (i) and (iii)

B (ii) and (iv)

C (v) and (vi)

D (ii) and (v)

E (i) and (iv)

F (iv) and (vi)

Passage Six

A Jolly Way to Kill Time

In this passage, Katie Grant, writing in The Scotsman *newspaper in March 2005, gives her views on the advantages and disadvantages of a "Gap Year".*

Read the passage straight through in order to get a general grasp of her attitude to Gap Years. Then answer the questions that follow.

1   As the mother of a gap-year student, I read with interest extracts of the study "Seeing the World: An Examination of Backpacking as a Global Youth Culture" by Lucy Huxley, a sociologist at Manchester Metropolitan University. Lucy Huxley may be a clever girl, for all I
5   know, but why it took her three years, and doubtless thousands of taxpayers' pounds, to discover that gap-year students may go abroad but, once there, hang about mostly with each other, phone home constantly and learn almost nothing about the country to which they have travelled, I do not know. Twenty-four hours in the home of a
10 gap-year student's parents would have shown her, more graphically than any study, what modern gap-yearing is all about.

In the main, it is about pretence: the pretence of independence. The advent of the e-mail has made that pretence increasingly difficult to uphold, but we do it anyway. Since our gap-year daughter is in Italy
15 and unlikely to read this, I will reveal, with a twinge of disloyalty, that scanning back through her e-mails, I know almost nothing of her life, but an awful lot about her bank account.

Recently, as I travelled on the train between Glasgow and Edinburgh, I found myself sitting behind a group of first-year
20 university students indulging in an exquisite (for the listener) game of one-upmanship over their gap-year travels. In those weary, God-I'm-sooooo-cool-I-can-hardly-speak voices, two young men and a young woman talked about bars they had visited in a country whose

name seemed to have escaped them – not that it mattered – and
25 how difficult it was to manage a hangover when the temperature
was 35°C. They laughed, again in their soooo-cool way, about
vomiting in the street of a town (un-named) among people (un-
named) who were "really soooo sweet".

Then they tried to outdo each other's tales of discomfort. I am sure
30 they thought all their fellow passengers were suitably impressed by
their gappie sophistication. Sadly, we were too polite to disabuse
them.

These young people illustrated only too clearly that, for most young
adults, gap years have become nothing more than a jolly way to kill
35 time. Nowadays, although gappies still return home with that oddly
endearing kind of youthful arrogance that declares them to have
been there, done that, as if that settled the matter, in fact, their year

➤

out no longer generates any real knowledge about anything, as the
path most of them have trodden is well-beaten and they mostly hang
40 out with each other.

It is claimed that students have a more productive time if they go to
countries on organised placements. But whereas this has some
advantages, if only to stop gap-year students wandering pointlessly
from bar to beach and back, it still does not quite produce the
45 independence of spirit, or the ability to cope with the unexpected
or the severance from the familiar that a gap year should ideally be
all about. If a gap-year student's greatest achievement is to have
followed the advice of some group leader on a pre-packaged
expedition to a specially-made jungle camp, or to have successfully
50 spent some months essentially playing at being a teacher in a third-
world village, all arranged through organisations such as Gap
Activity Projects, they will have had a wonderful time, and may even
have learned a skill or two, but it is hardly the stuff from which
heroes are made.

55 It would be unfair to tar all gappies with the same brush – some do
use their time productively – but it seems to me that gap years have
forfeited any claim to be an essential part of the maturing process.
For middle-class British students, the best that can be said is that a
gap year begins, very gently, to wean them away from the culture of
60 the risk assessment exercise and the health and safety checklist that
has cosseted them all their lives so far. Though insured to the last
strand of designer-straightened hair, gap-year students must, I hope,
take at least a smidgen more responsibility for themselves than they
did in their school sixth form.

65 I don't want to throw the baby out with the bathwater, however. If,
for middle-class English gappies, far from teaching them how to
combat loneliness and homesickness or opening their ears and eyes
to other cultures, the gap year has become little more than an early
introduction to corporate bonding, where the only lesson learned is

➢

70 how much they can drink under a baking sun, there are others who would benefit hugely.

When I was at Glasgow University (graduated 1997), far too many of my fellow students had scarcely been beyond the end of the road. The Scottish system, which sees students finishing school one term 75 and beginning "yooni" the next, in effect simply swapping the classroom for the lecture hall while still living at home and being looked after by their mothers, is as grim a recipe for parochialism of outlook as you could devise.

There are, I know, good financial reasons for this arrangement, 80 particularly with the four-year Scottish honours degree system. But it sets such a limit on the student's outlook on the world that it should be discouraged. University should be a faintly alarming experience. It should see students feeling, occasionally, that they have leaped out of a plane without a parachute. If Scottish students cannot afford 85 to live away from home during their university careers, a pre-university gap year, however pre-packaged, might provide some useful shock therapy. Moreover, if more Scottish students took a gap year, university dropout rates – currently rising – would drop, since those shovelled into the university system as statistical cannon-90 fodder would probably realise, as their horizons broadened, that "yooni" was not for them and find something else to do.

So while Lucy Huxley's study does prove something – that modern gap years lack a good shot of adrenalin, with spoon-feeding preferred to self-reliance – the gap year theory is still a good one, 95 even if the practice has gone soft.

Questions

I   In which paragraph does the writer state most clearly the benefits she thinks a gap year should provide for all students? (Identify the paragraph by line references.)

2 **(a)**   Which one of the following best describes the writer's attitude to Lucy Huxley's study as described in the first paragraph?

    A   She finds it interesting.

    B   She finds it amusing.

    C   She finds it frustrating.

    D   She finds it pointless.

    E   She finds it accurate.

  (b)   Which one of the following expressions in the first paragraph best conveys the contemptuous tone the writer uses when describing Lucy Huxley's work?

    A   "may be a clever girl"

    B   "for all I know"

    C   "took her three years"

    D   "doubtless thousands of taxpayers' pounds"

    E   "more graphically than any study"

3   Which one of the following best describes the writer's attitude to the students she encountered on the train journey (lines 18–32)?

    A   irritated

    B   angry

    C   amused

    D   saddened

    E   entertained

Questions

4 "I don't want to throw the baby out with the bathwater, however." (line 65)

Which of the following best explains what the writer means here?

A She doesn't want to criticise gap years so strongly that it appears there are no benefits.

B She doesn't want readers to think she is completely opposed to gap years.

C She doesn't want to appear unsympathetic to the positive side of gap years.

D She doesn't want to complain about middle class students' gap years only.

E She doesn't want to discourage Scottish students from taking gap years.

5 In lines 72–91 the writer argues that a gap year might be particularly beneficial for Scottish students. Which of the following is her main reason for this?

A The dropout rate in Scottish universities is high.

B Scottish students undertake a four year course.

C Most Scottish students live at home.

D Many Scottish students are not fully committed to university.

The Croc Hunter

Steve Irwin, nicknamed "The Croc Hunter", became famous for the TV documentaries he made about dangerous animals. In September 2006, while filming off the coast of Queensland, he was killed by a stingray. In The Scotsman a few days later, James Kirkup explains why he disapproves of Irwin's methods, and compares him with David Attenborough, also a maker of wildlife documentaries.

Read the passage straight through in order to get a general grasp of Kirkup's reasons for being critical of Irwin. Then answer the questions that follow.

1　I'm sorry, but I never had much time for Steve Irwin. All that leaping around, grabbing crocodiles, squeezing snakes and generally agitating whatever other fanged creature he could lay his hands on usually just made me wonder why he couldn't leave the poor brutes
5　alone, instead of apparently trying to provoke them to very visible displays of fear and anger.

　In part, it's probably just a generational thing: my childhood years left me with an untrammelled admiration for David Attenborough and a style of wildlife documentary film-making that leaves its
10　subjects as undisturbed as possible.

　Still, there's something here much more important than my nostalgia, which is how we see animals and how we treat them. The Croc Hunter's defenders would be quick to leap to his defence on this score, pointing out that Mr Irwin did a great deal to make us
15　more aware of animals, the need to preserve their habitats and generally assign more value to their wellbeing. And that's all valid stuff, as far as it goes.

➤

My problem is less with his methods than with his choice of subject matter. By focusing so relentlessly on the exciting, the entertaining,
20   the apex predators and other deadly killers, the noisy heirs to Attenborough are in grave danger of contributing to our growing collective ignorance about some far more numerous and, arguably, more important creatures and their condition.

As more and more people live and raise their children in towns and
25   cities, the countryside becomes more and more distant, a strange place to be driven through, flown over and only occasionally visited, and even then probably in the sanitised form of a stately home or a farmers' market. And since we city dwellers increasingly experience the world through a screen, documentaries which explain the
30   natural world to us are ever more important, helping us to form our ideas about animals and about the world that starts where the concrete ends.

Television shrinks distance, brings distant wonders into our homes and makes the extraordinary mundane. Anyone with a multichannel TV service has no trouble finding a wealth of the spectacular shows that are known in media circles as "shark porn": *The World's Deadliest Snakes*; *When Wolverines Attack*; *Killer Crustaceans* ... The list is endless, but the subject matter isn't, limited mainly to animals that can kill humans. Mr Irwin met his end filming a show entitled *Ocean's Deadliest* - something that even his biggest fans admit has to be a little ironic.

But what about the animals that humans kill? Scan the TV listings, the DVD racks and the work of Mr Irwin and the generation of imitators he spawned and you'll struggle to find anything that would give you a fair and balanced idea of how meat ends up your plate, or even what it looked like before it became meat.

It's no exaggeration to suggest that the average British child, whose exposure to animals other than domestic pets comes almost entirely from television, can probably name more types of shark and snake than breeds of sheep or cow. In their own way, Belted Galloways and Herdwicks have become more exotic and unknown than great whites and copperheads.

I'm willing to bet that the Border Union Agricultural Society's annual tup sale at Kelso this Friday will not be filmed and made into *When Sheep Go Bad*, an explosive 30-minute TV special on Sky Sharks Interactive Channel 27. It may be the biggest ram sale in Europe, with millions of pounds changing hands, but for all that, and no matter how dramatically the more energetic beasts butt one another or try to leap out of the pens, sheep aren't exciting.

But that doesn't mean they're not important. The notion that, when it comes to animals, excitement = importance, is a singularly unhelpful one, but it is a formula that Mr Irwin's work did a great deal to promote. It just leads us further down the baleful road of

➤

65 ignoring the "boring" animals that we routinely raise, slaughter and
eat.

And it's not just TV stars who are guilty of this, by the way. The media
generally are culpable: how many mainstream news stories about
farms and farm animals don't involve some element of disease-based
scaremongering, from foot and mouth to mad cow disease to bird flu?

70 There's another interesting side-effect of the veneration of exotic,
exciting and endangered species too, which is to overdevelop our
protective urges towards animals, because if you're repeatedly told
that animals are precious, rare and fragile things that must be
preserved (and some undoubtedly are), then it's that little bit harder
75 to accept that some animals exist only because we're going to kill and
eat them. How many people today can either not bear to eat meat at
all, or only eat it without admitting to themselves that it was alive
before it ended up in that sterile plastic box on the supermarket shelf?

Anyone who eats meat and fully accepts that it was once a living,
80 breathing cow, pig, sheep, whatever, should take a keen interest in
how that animal was raised and treated. It's only by buying high-
quality meat which has come from reliable, considerate farmers, by
accepting the higher price that entails, and by rejecting cheap,
"factory farmed" produce, that we can hope to encourage good
85 farming practice and drive out the bad. Closing your eyes to the
origins of meat and simply going for the lowest price available will
only hand profits to those who don't treat their animals as well as
they could.

I'm sure Steve Irwin was a decent man who cared about animals and
90 thought he was doing important work showing a generation of
children the wonders of crocs, snakes and all the other exhilarating,
dangerous beasties he wrestled. But he'd have done a lot more good
if he'd introduced them to some even more fantastical creatures:
sheep, cows, pigs, chickens . . .

Questions

1 Re-read lines 1–23.

Which one of the following statements best explain the writer's reason for preferring Attenborough to Irwin?

A Irwin doesn't respect animals.

B He is nostalgic about Attenborough.

C Attenborough doesn't concentrate on "exciting" animals.

D Attenborough merely observes the animals.

E Irwin makes the animals afraid and aggressive.

2 Re-read lines 24–69.

In lines 29–30 Kirkup states: "… documentaries which explain the natural world to us are ever more important".

(a) Which of the following best explains why he believes this:

  A Not enough people are interested in the natural world.

  B TV documentaries are a good way of learning.

  C Modern lifestyle means there is less contact with the natural world.

  D People watch a lot of TV.

(b) Which of the following best describes his criticism of what the makers of TV documentaries actually do:

  A They make documentaries with aggressive sounding titles.

  B They ignore events like the tup sale at Kelso.

  C They give the impression that only exciting animals are important.

  D They present a negative image of animals.

  E They leave children knowing almost nothing about farm animals.

3 The main point in lines 70–88 is:

A More people would become vegetarians if the knew how meat was prepared.

B We know very little about how farm animals are raised.

C We'd rather not think about meat as once having been a living animal.

D If we eat meat, we should support farmers who treat their animals well.

Questions

4 In the last paragraph (lines 89–94) the writer's attitude to Irwin is rather contemptuous. Which of the following has the strongest influence in creating this tone?

    A calling him a "decent" man

    B saying he "thought" he was doing important work

    C using informal words such as "crocs" and "beasties"

    D starting the last sentence with "But"

    E saying he could have done "a lot more good"

Friends Reunited

The website "Friends Reunited" became very popular in the early years of the 21st century. It allows people to make contact with former classmates from school and to exchange information with them.

The passage below, which appeared in The Herald *newspaper in January 2003, is by Melanie Reid, at that time a regular writer of "opinion" pieces for that paper. Read the passage straight through in order to get a general grasp of Reid's attitude to the website and the people who use it. Then answer the questions that follow.*

1   The moment you log on to the Friends Reunited website, as an estimated 15,000–20,000 people do every day, you embark on a strange kind of anthropology: a journey into your own past. There you will find people whose names you vaguely recognise, and
5   encounter long-forgotten memories: whiffs of floor polish or mouldy hockey boots; the slam of desk lids. There, among the ghosts of your school days, you will find a simplicity and a certainty about who you once were.

     If ever anyone wanted proof that nostalgia sells, Friends Reunited is
10   it. The website, which now has eight million subscribers, has been the phenomenon of internet-age Britain. With more members than there are trades unionists, and fast catching up with the Automobile Association's 12 million members, Friends Reunited has become one of the biggest organisations in the country in just over two years.

15   Like all hugely successful ideas, it couldn't have been simpler: offer a national message board for old school friends who may not have seen each other for 20 years or more. Now 45,000 schools are listed, and anyone can log on, read about other people, post an update on their own lives, and for a small fee, make contact.

➤

20　Most people are happy just to chat about themselves. The website's "success board" and "school memories" lists are filled with enthusiastic stories, happy events, self-conscious jokes (and a plethora of exclamation marks). "I had a wonderful time at both reunions, and would like to invite anyone from the class of 1964 to
25　get in touch." "A very old and close friend of mine found me though your website. We lost touch 20 years ago." "Miss Greaves – we nailed a rotten kipper under her desk and she took hours to find it!!!" "We played American skipping which was with elastic bands joined together: does anyone remember that?"

30　Friends Reunited has a compulsive quality: it defies human nature to log on and then not to peek at the list of your own contemporaries. So it was that, in researching this piece, I was unable to resist opening a door to my past to find an entry from a small boy I once carried aloft in piggyback fights at primary school, whose entry is

35 fairly typical of a million others: "Married for 20 years (to the same person!). Two daughters 12 and 9 (late starter!). Still living in town (really boring!). Still playing rugby (bloody mad!!). I am a maths teacher (really bloody mad!!!!)."

You can see what I mean about the exclamation marks. Read
40 between the lines and you perceive a decent, self-deprecating man who, for all his self-consciousness about doing it, can't help reaching out into the ether to see what the past can offer him. He's needy. He's fishing for who knows what: camaraderie, recognition, excitement, adventure. There are millions like him. Friends Reunited
45 is as sad, trite, silly, nosey, mundane, and boastful as it is sweet, warm, life-enhancing, diverse and poignant. It is a mirror held up to our lives.

It succeeds because it taps into the world of school, the ultimate shared experience. But I suspect the unconscious brilliance of the
50 website is what it says about contemporary society. It is, above all, a thing of its time. Children who grew up in gentler, securer times are now adults grappling with a difficult world. Communities which used to be tight are now scattered. This is an age of mobility: marital, social, and geographical. People are widely dispersed and frequently
55 estranged from their roots.

Take it to the extreme, and Friends Reunited symbolises the amount of chronic loneliness that exists as a result. This is a competitive, high-speed, relentless age. We don't have time or opportunity to find people, or talk to them, or develop friendships: no wonder we
60 love a website, bathed in the warm light of nostalgia, which does it for us. It is, in its spectacularly simple way, pub, club, network, professional association, singles night, missing person's bureau, and dating agency all rolled into one.

As dating agency it has led to many romances – but it has already
65 gained infamy as a breaker of marriages. In case after case, reunions

➤

provoked by the website have led to steamy affairs between adults desperate to rekindle the spark of youth. Unconsummated teenage romances have exploded into life again, with dire consequences. After my own ghastly 25th school reunion, which took place shortly
70 before Friends Reunited started, there was a subsequent outbreak of sexual liaisons between all kinds of highly respectable married lawyers and accountants and executives; and to my knowledge at least one divorce resulted from it.

But all this just adds to the emptiness that underpins Friends
75 Reunited once you get beyond the essential fascination. You make contact with people you were at school with. You exchange names, e-mails, and career stories. Then what? You will come to realise that the expectation of meeting these people again was far more pleasurable than the reality. Slowly it dawns on you that the reason
80 you didn't keep in touch with them in the first place was because you had nothing in common with them; and there is no earthly reason why you should feel any closer to them now 20 years have passed. Once you have exchanged life stories, and gained recognition for your career achievements, shared a few old jokes
85 about teachers, and showed them pictures of your children, then very often there is little else to say. The only half-decent thing left to do is that refuge of the dead relationship: the Christmas card which says "Must see you this year" and means the opposite.

Everything is nicer in the past. Safer. It is human nature to seek
90 comfort and reassurance there. Friends Reunited can be seen as wish fulfilment for millions of 30 and 40 and 50 somethings who feel their lives have not turned out to be quite as they hoped. It speaks of times when things were simpler, easier, sexier, happier. It is, perhaps, a new version of Peter Pan for a new century.

Questions

1   Which one of the following statements best sums up the writer's main point about why the Friends Reunited website is so popular?

   A   It reminds people of happier times.

   B   It has a huge number of members.

   C   It provides an escape form the realities of middle-aged life.

   D   It causes people to start exciting new relationships.

   E   It allows people to make contact and exchange memories of school.

2   Which of the following statements best describes the writer's feelings about the website?

   A   It is intriguing.

   B   It is entertaining.

   C   It is dangerous.

   D   It is shallow.

   E   It is reassuring.

3   Do you think the reference to "Peter Pan" in the final sentence is meant to be:

   A   complimentary about the website

   B   uncomplimentary about the website

   C   neither complimentary nor uncomplimentary about the website

Fools, Damned Fools, and "Experts"

In this passage, from *The Sunday Times* newspaper, *novelist and journalist India Knight takes a look at people's reliance on so-called experts. She begins with a reference to a TV health "expert" who had been criticised for calling herself "Doctor".*

Read the passage straight through to get a general idea of Knight's views on "experts" and the tone she adopts when describing them. Then answer the questions that follow.

1   "Doctor" Gillian McKeith, the unhealthy looking "health guru" who humiliates fat people on television, last week agreed to drop the "Doctor" part of her name in advertisements. This followed an investigation by the Advertising Standards Authority, which had
5   come to the preliminary conclusion that the use of the word was likely to mislead the public. It's not the first time that McKeith has been censured by regulators and there seems to be a question mark over the validity of some of her qualifications. Ben Goldacre, the journalist and (real) doctor, pointed out last week that his dead cat,
10   Hettie, was, like McKeith, a "certified professional member" of the American Association of Nutritional Consultants, the membership having been bought online for $60.

What's interesting about this is how willing people are to suspend disbelief when it comes to "improving" themselves. I look at
15   McKeith and I think, "If eating like you means looking as unwell as you, thanks, but no thanks."

Presumably this isn't that wildly unusual a reaction – I mean, we all have eyes. And yet people appear to be queuing up to be humiliated by her on television, told that their insides are like cesspits and

                                                  ➤

20 worse and have their excrement examined in public. Perhaps
they're just desperate – in which case it seems unkind, to put it
mildly, to reduce some of them to tears of shame and self-disgust on
national television.

But anyway, my point is: whatever happened to instinct? Do
25 hundreds of thousands of people really need to be told how to eat –
to be told that guzzling vast quantities of chips is bad for you, or that
drinking water is better than drinking the fluorescent fizzy stuff? I
don't want to sound hypocritical here, having just written a diet
book, but I do think that the reason why the book has done well is
30 that my co-author and I make no claims of expertise whatsoever –
quite the contrary, in fact. The approach is clearly not without appeal.

Yet elsewhere the public's appetite for "experts" seems insatiable.
People who have babies get their knickers in the most terrible twist,

agonising over which "childcare expert" they should turn to for
35 advice. In some childcare experts' hands, a three-month-old baby is
no longer just a sweet little baby but a difficult and demanding
creature that must be bossed into conforming to certain parent-
pleasing patterns – instead of being left in peace to get on with its
own baby-pleasing little routine of sleeping, eating, filling nappies
40 and being kissed.

Once that's happened, the poor old baby is quite likely to be dragged
from one "expert" to another during its infancy – something that
would be understandable if the child were ill, but that makes no
sense at all given that it's healthy. And yet here they come: the
45 osteopaths, the naturopaths, the homeopaths, the baby massage
"experts", the child nutritionists, the sleep advisers, on and on. It's
like a parallel universe populated by mad people. And yet the parents
all have instincts, which they have decided not to trust. Why?

In some quarters I'm sure this loony kind of behaviour is born out of
50 love – out of wanting one's child to have the best of everything and
not taking any chances. But the end result is overcoddling to the
point that an older child, already worked incredibly hard at school,
doesn't have time to play outside in the evening because of
homework, music, drama, fencing, astrophysics, and so on.

55 Whatever happened to running about prodding things with sticks
and getting muddy? And then, of course, when the child rightly
rebels against this hothousing onslaught – showing, at least, that its
spirit hasn't been entirely crushed – its well-meaning parents call in
the child psychologist. Because they trust an expert and they don't
60 trust themselves.

They're everywhere, the experts. We can't cook any more,
apparently – we need armies of people telling us how to address the
problematic question of vegetables. We can't have relationships
without ludicrous self-help books in which complete strangers,

65 usually American, usually low on charm, tell you very specifically what to say or not to say to your boyfriend. It's all very well making fun of them – I wish we'd do it more often – but these books, DVDs, guides and manuals sell by the million.

What's wrong with us? We can't even have sex. You'd think it
70 wasn't that complicated and that in this department, if in no other, instinct might take over but apparently it's not simple at all. It's rocket science and we need TV shows to tell us how we're doing it wrong, more guidebooks, more "experts". It's like a collective form of extreme hypochondria.

75 What I'd really like to know – unfortunately, there's no research available that I can find – is whether this Niagara of "expert advice" actually improves anyone's quality of life. From my observations, it just makes people anxious, stressed and dissatisfied. I could be wrong but our collective willingness to suspend disbelief and to
80 dole out large sums for the privilege of "expert" advice would suggest some problem with self-esteem. Are we really that lost? Is everything really that confusing?

It would seem so. Our own opinions count for nothing until they have been backed up by some random bogus person banging on
85 about "research" and "findings". We clearly feel that life is, or ought to be, reducible to a series of instructions, a bit like a self-assembly bookcase from Ikea, and that we couldn't possibly work out the instructions for ourselves using a mixture of instinct and experience. Like needy children, we need approbation at every turn.

90 Expertise used to be interesting. You'd listen, frowning with concentration, as some boffin on BBC2 explained some otherwise impenetrable piece of complicated science, and you'd go to bed feeling you'd learnt something. That still happens, thank God, but real experts have become the minority. These days everyone's an
95 expert: no subject is too small, too insignificant or too ridiculous – and no qualification too bogus.

Questions

1 Which one of the following statements best sums up the writer's main reason for disapproving of "experts"?

   A Many of them have bogus qualifications.

   B Their advice is often contradictory.

   C They are only in it for the money.

   D We should rely on our own common sense.

   E There are far too many of them.

2 The writer begins with a reference to a specific "expert" and then opens the argument out to deal with "experts" in general. At what point in the passage does this "turning point" occur?

   A lines 13–14 ("What's interesting … themselves.")

   B line 24 ("But anyway … instinct?")

   C line 32 ("Yet elsewhere … insatiable.")

   D line 61 ("They're everywhere, the experts.")

3 The writer makes frequent use of humour in this passage. Rank the following examples in order of how humorous you find them as they are used in the passage.

   A "his dead cat, Hettie, was, like McKeith, a 'certified professional member' of the American Association of Nutritional Consultants" (lines 9–11)

   B "get on with its own baby-pleasing little routine of sleeping, eating, filling nappies and being kissed" (lines 38–40)

   C "It's like a parallel universe populated by mad people." (lines 46–47)

   D "because of homework, music, drama, fencing, astrophysics, and so on" (lines 53–54)

Questions

4 "Do hundreds of thousands of people really need to be told how to eat – to be told that guzzling vast quantities of chips is bad for you, or that drinking water is better than drinking the fluorescent fizzy stuff?" (lines 24–27)

(a) Which one of the following words most clearly conveys the writer's contempt for the activity she is describing?

A "guzzling"

B "vast"

C "quantities"

D "chips"

(b) Which one of the following words most clearly conveys the writer's contempt for the drink she is describing?

A "fluorescent"

B "fizzy"

C "stuff"

5 "this Niagara of 'expert advice'" (line 76)

By comparing it with the Niagara Falls, which **two** of the following does the writer probably want to bring to mind to support her criticism of "expert advice"?

A enormous size

B unstoppable force

C extreme noise

D capacity to drown

E destructive power

The Celebrity Circus

Writing in The Scotsman *newspaper in February 2003, broadcaster and journalist Joyce Macmillan examines the subject of celebrity and its impact on our lives. She refers to a recent Film and TV awards ceremony and to a court case in which a celebrity couple were suing a magazine. The reference to "these worrying times" in lines 4–5 is to the imminent war in Iraq.*

Read the passage straight through to get a general grasp of the writer's feelings about celebrities and about the importance they have in many people's lives. Then answer the questions that follow.

1   The BAFTA awards ceremony in London on Sunday must have come as a small godsend to the media in a week full of serious news; it is, after all, the kind of daft, glitzy and glittery showbiz event that might have been designed to provide a touch of light relief in these
5   worrying times. The celebs were all there, of course, flashing their latest designer gear - the Nicole Kidmans and the Renee Zellwegers, the Michael Caines and the Meryl Streeps.

And at the eye of the storm - where she seems to love to be - was the gorgeous Catherine Zeta Jones, screen goddess and wicked lady
10   extraordinary.

Fresh from last week's High Court appearance in her lawsuit against *Hello!* magazine for publishing pirated photographs of her wedding reception, Zeta Jones pocketed the prize for best supporting actress, yelled "Oggy oggy oggy, oi oi oi" to her family back in Swansea, and
15   naturally found herself the object of some hostile attention from the media.

It was, in other words, all good knockabout stuff; but there are reasons, all the same, why we should pause to think a little harder

➤

about the frenzied intensity of modern celebrity culture, and the
20 huge role it has come to play in millions of lives. There have always
been celebrities and famous folk, of course; and we have always
gossiped and speculated about them. But the colossal growth of the
mass media throughout the 20th century turned the creation and
marketing of celebrity into a multi-billion dollar global industry; and
25 this change took place at a moment when our whole society was
moving from a world governed by traditional and community values
to a world generally governed by market and commercial values, in
which people are more mobile and more autonomous, but are also
lonelier and more bereft of a sense of community.

30 Into that void of shared human experience the media have
obligingly poured this whole community of imaginary friends and
acquaintances, the film stars and soap stars, the Big Brother
housemates and the transient pop idols. And in that sense, the

satirist Chris Morris was right when he suggested that all some
35 terrorists would have to do, if they wanted to disorientate our
society completely, would be to "take out" the few hundred leading
celebrities who fill the pages of our celebrity magazines and tabloid
press every week, since they provide our society with its main point
of convergence, its shared topic of conversation, and its leading
40 source of entertainment.

Nor is there any point in denying that some aspects of this celebrity
culture are vicious, and even potentially fascistic. In a remarkable
play called "Stones in His Pockets" by the Belfast writer Marie Jones,
two performers, alone on stage, act out the story of what happens
45 when a Hollywood movie crew comes to film in a depressed small
town in the west of Ireland. The play's tragic climax comes when
one of the most vulnerable kids in the village is thrown out of his
own local pub by a team of security heavies for the offence of trying
to say "hello" to the gorgeous female star of the movie, who is
50 slumming it for the evening. And there's something about this
situation that exposes the hidden brutalism of celebrity culture with
terrific force. In a world where people have become commodities,
the play seems to say, some can earn millions a month simply for
hanging around being themselves, while others have no value or
55 rights at all; and this is a human tragedy not only for the losers – and
for millions of ordinary kids driven mad by improbable dreams of
fame and fortune – but also for the winners.

Which brings me back to the Zeta Jones court case, and the
extraordinary collision of values it represents. On one hand, Zeta
60 Jones and her film-star husband want to argue that they are human
beings with a right to privacy in their family life, and that no-one
should photograph their wedding celebrations without their
consent. Yet on the other hand, they are so used to parcelling
themselves up and selling themselves as a celebrity package –
65 romance, marriage, lifestyle, baby and all – that they had already, at
the time when the illicit snapper was hard at it at the wedding, done

a lucrative deal with the rival *OK!* magazine to publish dozens of pages of authorised pictures of the same star-studded event. Whatever the outcome of the case, this contradiction in their
70 position has left them looking greedy, self-indulgent and ridiculous.

But perhaps not much more ridiculous than the rest of us, who happily condemn them for their hypocrisy, but continue to buy the magazines in which their images appear. For in the end, the only way to combine a reasonable interest in the lives of the rich and
75 famous with a decent sense of personal worth and dignity is to live in a society which genuinely holds to the belief that all human beings are of equal worth, and which not only talks the talk of equal rights, but also makes some effort to walk the walk.

And at the moment, our society – with our consent – is
80 comprehensively failing to do so. Our rhetoric is egalitarian and democratic, of course, but our behaviour is increasingly feudal, submissive, voyeuristic, particularly towards this new super-rich global aristocracy. It's as if, like the peasantry of old, we have actually begun to revert to the belief that wealth and fame is a mark
85 of divine favour and superior worth.

To have stars and role-models is healthy enough within reason, but to allow the full magic of life, its beauty and glamour, to become the preserve of a chosen few rather than the birthright of every boy and girl – that, it seems to me, as I watch the celebrity circus pass by, is
90 a profoundly undemocratic impulse.

Questions

1   According to the passage as a whole, which one of the following aspects of "modern celebrity culture" does the writer find most disturbing?

   A   the amount of money some celebrities make

   B   the way celebrity distorts our belief in equality

   C   the extent of celebrity coverage in the media

   D   the hypocrisy of some celebrities

   E   the fact that we all accept the influence of celebrities

2   "There have always been celebrities and famous folk, of course; and we have always gossiped and speculated about them." What, according to lines 17–40, is different now? Choose what you consider be the writer's main point.

   A   the mass media have increased hugely

   B   society is less community-based

   C   we would be lost without celebrities

   D   people move around more

   E   celebrity is a huge worldwide business

3   In lines 41–57 the writer uses her account of the play "Stones in His Pockets" to illustrate her belief that "some aspects of this celebrity culture are vicious, and even potentially fascistic". Which one of the following expressions from that paragraph comes closest to helping you understand what she means, in this context, by "fascistic"?

   A   "thrown out … by security heavies"

   B   "the hidden brutalism"

   C   "with terrific force"

   D   "people have become commodities"

   E   "no value or rights at all"

Questions

4 What is the "contradiction" to which the writer refers in line 69 when referring to the court case brought by Zeta Jones and her husband?

    A They are rich but wanted money for their wedding photographs.

    B They took money from one magazine for photographs but sued another for publishing them.

    C They are famous but wanted to prevent publication of their wedding photographs.

    D They claimed the right to privacy but sold the rights to their wedding photographs.

5 Which of the following is the main point being made in the last three paragraphs (lines 71–90)?

    A We think of ourselves as democratic but allow celebrities to have a special status.

    B We criticise celebrities but go on buying the publications they appear in.

    C We live in a modern world but behave as if we were peasants.

    D We give celebrities a lot of respect but everyone deserves this.

What Homeschooling Taught Me

In this passage Ben Macintyre, writing in *The Times* newspaper, *recalls his brief experience of "homeschooling" – when his parents took him out of school and educated him themselves. He goes on to consider the pros and cons of the whole idea of homeschooling.*

Read the passage straight through to get a general picture of Macintyre's year of homeschooling and get a general grasp of his attitude to it now. Then answer the questions that follow.

1   When I was eight years old, my parents chose to take me out of the state education system and teach me themselves. There were several factors behind this decision – practical, personal and ideological. My father had a year's sabbatical from university teaching and he and my
5   mother wanted to take the family to live in a cottage in the Scottish Highlands. Since the place was miles from the nearest school, they decided that the best way to continue my education, and that of my ten-year-old sister, would be to go it alone. I think they relished the challenge of a little do-it-yourself child-moulding, but another reason
10   for opting out of the system for a while was my growing aversion to school. I wasn't being bullied and I was not falling that far below the low standard expected at my averagely dismal school in England; but I was bored witless, and increasingly rebellious.

So in April 1972, we loaded up the battered Peugeot with home-
15   teaching manuals, paper, pencils, a mini-blackboard, and a copy of *Food for Free*, the bible for devotees of wild mushrooms and other natural edibles. (My parents were then going through a fungal stage and were determined to live partly off the land.) Thus began a brief but intensive diet of home education and dodgy toadstools.

20   At the time, most friends of my parents regarded the decision to

educate us in a hilltop bothy without electricity, telephone or television as, at best, eccentric, and at worst downright irresponsible. Today, by contrast, home education is booming as never before: parents worried by dropping school standards, exam
25 pressure and, above all, bullying are removing their children from mainstream schools in record numbers. According to Education Otherwise, the support group for home educators, at least 170,000 children are being taught at home, with 20,000 parents taking their children out of school in the past year alone.

30 The home-schooling debate is intense and complex, since so much depends on the needs of individual children, and the dedication of individual parents. Supporters insist that home education allows children and parents to bond while exploring an infinite and unfettered range of subject-matter; statistics show that home-
35 educated children go on to do well at university and in later life.

Critics point out that home-schooled children risk being cocooned from the beneficial social stresses of school life and are deprived of the opportunities offered by a more traditional educational community.

40 My period of home education lasted less than a year and was never intended to be permanent. Although we stuck roughly to the national syllabus, other aspects of the home-school regime were idiosyncratic. Lessons began early and ended at lunchtime, the rest of the day being devoted to what my parents called "environmental

45 studies" – to the outside world this probably looked more like "sailing", or "beetle collecting" or simply "getting very grubby". I built a Roman catapult and a milk churn, and dammed the burn with such success that I flooded the neighbour's field. I learned to knit. We invented our own amusements, such as tying my little brother to

50 the pet sheep which then bucked until he fell off, a sport we called "mutton busting".

With one-on-one tuition, we seemed to race through the subjects on the syllabus and set books at record speed, with the exception of mathematics, which my parents found almost as baffling as I did; the

55 maths lessons quietly lapsed. When it stopped raining and the sun came out, which I seem to recall happened rarely, school was immediately cancelled. Lessons were also abandoned during sheep-shearing, Test matches on the radio and when my father decreed that the climatic conditions were favourable for a fishing expedition.

60 But being taught under a parental microscope was hard work, and sometimes fraught; the blurring of the parent-teacher distinction led to some spectacular confrontations. My parents dutifully set us end-of-term exams, which we usually refused to do, or else cheated at abominably. I was capable of throwing an all-day wobbly over the

65 mildest criticism. With few other children to play with, I grew very close to my siblings, but we fought like ferrets in a sack. I would like to pretend that we were always absorbed in this idyllic world of

mists and moorland and improving works of literature, but we were not. I felt the lack of television like a missing limb.

70　When the time came to return to formal schooling in the autumn, my parents were exhausted: the experiment had been rewarding, they said in retrospect, but they showed no inclination to repeat it. After a semi-feral existence, I was delighted to wear a uniform again, and I gorged myself on television. But the experience had given me 75　an interest and confidence in learning I had never had before.

Home education is not a panacea. If schools were better, and bullying less prevalent, then far fewer parents would even consider it. But for some children home education works, producing balanced, well-rounded adults who might never thrive in traditional 80　schools. This is not some hippy fad, or the preserve of over-ambitious hot-housing parents, but a genuine alternative for those with the energy and patience to try it.

I suppose I romanticise my foray into home education, but it has left me, more than 30 years on, with some hilarious and happy 85　memories, and the conviction that there is more than one way to teach a child. Today I can still identify every variety of edible fungus in Scotland; on the other hand, I have never mastered my times tables.

Questions

1   In the first two paragraphs (lines 1–19) what impression is the writer trying to give of his parents?

   A They were being selfish.

   B They were slightly eccentric.

   C They were badly organised.

   D They were being over-protective.

   E They were highly opinionated.

2   Re-read lines 20–39. Which one of the following best sums up the writer's attitude, in these lines only, to homeschooling:

   A strong support

   B limited support

   C neither support nor criticism

   D limited criticism

   E strong criticism

3   "… other aspects of the home-school regime were idiosyncratic …" (lines 42–43)

   From a reading of lines 43–51, choose one of the following as the best definition of "idiosyncratic".

   A enjoyable

   B varied

   C peculiar

   D chaotic

   E unconventional

4   What impression is given in lines 70–75 of the Macintyre family's homeschooling experience?

   A very positive

   B a little bit positive

   C neutral

   D a little bit negative

   E very negative

Questions

5 In his conclusion (lines 76–88) what is Macintyre's final opinion of homeschooling?

    A strong support

    B limited support

    C neither support nor criticism

    D limited criticism

    E strong criticism

TV Soaps

The book TV Soaps *by Richard Kilborn, published in 1992, is an academic study of the construction and enduring appeal of Soap Operas on TV. In this extract from the opening chapter, the writer looks at various attitudes to their popularity and tries to find some reasons for it.*

Read the passage straight through to establish Kilborn's views and the attitudes he takes to others' points of view. Then answer the questions that follow.

1　About the popularity of television soaps there can be no doubt. As a topic of everyday conversation in home, office or classroom, talk about the latest twist in a story-line or a momentous event in the life of a well-known soap character provides a rich source for constant
5　and enthusiastic conjecture.

Many reasons have been advanced to explain the continuing – and some would say rather alarming – fascination that soaps have for such a large number, but one of the most persuasive is that they allow particularly strong bonds to develop between characters and
10　audience. These bonds sometimes become so strong that some viewers feel personally implicated in what happens in the lives of these characters; to the extent that an attempt by the production team to kill off certain characters is often met with vigorous audience protest. What seems to happen is that over a period of
15　time viewers regard soap characters, or even the whole programme, as having moved into the public domain.

Various explanations have been offered for the tenacity with which viewers cling to or identify with characters in soaps. One of those frequently advanced is that audiences find it possible to relate to
20　these fictional creations in ways often denied them in their real-life

relationships. It is almost as if – in an age where an increasing number of people have lost that sustaining sense of belonging to a community, a neighbourhood or even a family group – the possibility of regular involvement in the lives and affairs of a fictional
25 group or community can be a very attractive one. Psychologists might even claim that such ongoing attachment can be positively beneficial, as it fulfils a compensatory function.

In spite of the evident pleasure which soaps bring to so many viewers on such a regular basis, there have been no small number of
30 people who have been only too ready to pour scorn on what they see as a highly dubious phenomenon. Such critics regard soaps as representing some of the worst excesses of popular television and take exception to what they perceive to be a particularly addictive and mindless form of entertainment. For those who take this view,
35 soaps are simply a waste of time, mere "chewing gum for the eyes",

not particularly offensive in themselves, but guilty of diverting viewers from more challenging and intellectually stimulating types of cultural activity.

In addition to those who take this frankly elitist approach, there are
40 others who believe that soaps can be a positively harmful, if not corrupting, influence. Consumers of certain soaps will – according to these self-appointed moral watchdogs – be tempted to model their own behaviour on the words and deeds of some of the fictional characters they regularly encounter. The argument is that since
45 what is heard and seen in soaps often falls far short of being exemplary or inspiring, who can be surprised if we witness in real life an increasing amount of violent and anti-social, if not downright criminal, behaviour.

Small wonder – in view of the generally low esteem in which soaps
50 are held – that over the years a number of quite potent myths have emerged about what watching soaps can do to you. People have been made to feel that a long-term commitment to their favourite soap opera was equivalent to a dangerous addiction. The result has been that for some viewers an innocent and pleasurable activity, in
55 which there is a high degree of emotional involvement, has become tinged with distinctly guilty feelings. As a consequence of this, many people have not always felt able to admit the pleasures they gain from soaps, for fear that friends and neighbours would think less of them for wasting their time on such trivia.

60 Attempting to pinpoint the particular pleasures which soap-watching can provide is not an easy task, but based on the findings of viewer surveys, one can begin to establish certain broad categories. First, and possibly foremost, there is the pleasure of continuing involvement, the anticipation that at a set time and on a
65 regular basis one will be invited into a world about which one has acquired – often over a long period of time – a considerable amount of pleasure. The contours of the soap opera world become in many

ways as familiar as those which constitute one's everyday reality. The characters who play major roles in this fictional world are thus
70 able to become the equivalent of friends or acquaintances. In fact some viewers will conduct imaginary conversations with these characters at times when they need comfort or advice, or even resort to writing to them when the character needs to be warned that something untoward is about to happen. All this is proof of the
75 extent to which soaps can tap into people's imaginative and emotional lives and of the vicarious pleasure or pain which viewers can experience as a result of their long-term involvement with characters.

If one of the pleasures of soap watching derives from a strong sense
80 of involvement, a further source of enjoyment is the endless speculation which a serial encourages among its followers. Most fictional narratives are organised in order to promote feelings of expectation or tension, but soaps are particularly adept at stimulating many forms of conjecture. How will a character respond
85 when he or she is given a piece of news to which we, as viewers, are already privy? How long will it be before the character X finds out about Y's infidelity? And what chance does Z have of ever fully recovering from that blow on the head which has led to such severe amnesia? Questions such as these form recurrent components of
90 soap narratives and the promise that next week's episode will go some way to resolving these uncertainties is part of the unwritten contract between the producers and the audience. This is the very heart of soaps' continuing fascination.

Questions

1 Which one of the following best describes the main focus of the first three paragraphs (lines 1–27)?

   A The wide popularity of TV Soaps

   B The dangers of watching TV Soaps

   C The idea that viewers identify with characters in TV Soaps

   D The benefits of watching TV Soaps

   E The idea that TV Soaps are a substitute for community and family life

   F The reasons for the popularity of TV Soaps

2 Re-read paragraphs 4 and 5 (lines 28–48).

(a) Paragraph 4 (lines 28–38) looks at the criticisms made by one group of people who disapprove of TV Soaps. Which one of the following adjectives describes what seems to be their main criticism of TV Soaps?

   A "dubious" (line 31)

   B "addictive" (line 33)

   C "mindless" (line 34)

   D "offensive" (line 36)

   E "guilty" (line 36)

(b) Paragraph 5 (lines 39–48) looks at the criticisms of a second group of people who disapprove of TV Soaps. Which one of the following is **not** a belief held by this group?

   A There is a connection between the amount of violence in TV Soaps and the amount of violence in real life.

   B People who watch TV Soaps sometimes copy the behaviour of characters in the programmes.

   C Characters in TV Soaps are not good role models.

   D People who watch TV Soaps need protection from bad influences.

   E People who watch TV Soaps are an inferior type of person.

Questions

3 The sentence "If one of the pleasures of soap watching derives from a strong sense of involvement, a further source of enjoyment is the endless speculation which a serial encourages among its followers" (lines 79–81) acts as a **link sentence** between the last two paragraphs.

   (a) Which of the expressions quoted in A to F below **refer back** to the subject matter of lines 60–78?

   (b) Which of the expressions quoted in A to F below **refer forward** to the subject matter of lines 81–93?

   A "pleasures of soap watching"

   B "sense of involvement"

   C "a further source of enjoyment"

   D "endless speculation"

   E "a serial encourages"

   F "among its followers"

4 Indicate whether each of the following quotations from the passage is

   A an expression of the writer's own opinion

   or

   B someone else's opinion being conveyed to us by the writer

   (i) "… can be positively beneficial …" (lines 26–27)

   (ii) "… the worst excesses of popular television …" (line 32)

   (iii) "… frankly elitist approach …" (line 39)

   (iv) "… self-appointed moral watchdogs …" (line 42)

   (v) "… a dangerous addiction…" (line 53)

   (vi) "… an innocent and pleasurable activity …" (line 54)

5 Which one of the following words is **not** being used metaphorically in the passage:

   A "cling" (line 18)

   B "pour" (line 30)

   C "myths" (line 50)

   D "pinpoint" (line 60)

   E "contours" (line 67)

A Hundred Years of the Aeroplane

On the 17th of December 2003 there were celebrations to mark the 100th anniversary of the aeroplane. The celebrations focused on the town of Kitty Hawk in North Carolina, USA, which was where the flying machine designed by brothers Orville and Wilbur Wright was first successfully flown.

The passage below, which appeared as an article in The Guardian *newspaper on 16 December 2003, was written by George Monbiot, a well-known environmentalist. Read the passage straight through in order to get a general grasp of Monbiot's point of view. Then answer the questions that follow.*

1   They will probably be commemorating the wrong people in Kitty Hawk, North Carolina, tomorrow. Five months before the Wright brothers lifted a flying machine into the air for 12 seconds above the sand dunes, a New Zealander, Richard Pearse, had travelled for more
5   than a kilometre in his contraption, without the help of ramps or slides, and had even managed to turn his plane in mid-flight.

But history belongs to those who record it, so tomorrow is the official centenary of the aeroplane. At Kitty Hawk, the President of the United States will deliver a eulogy to aviation, while a number of
10   men with more money than sense will seek to recreate the Wrights' first flight. Well, they can keep their anniversary. Tomorrow should be a day of international mourning. December 17 2003 is the centenary of the world's most effective killing machine.

The aeroplane was not the first weapon of mass destruction. The
15   European powers had already learned to rain terror upon their colonial subjects by means of naval bombardment, artillery and machine guns. But the destructive potential of aerial bombing had

been grasped even before the first plane left the ground. In 1886, Jules Verne imagined aircraft acting as a global police force, bombing barbaric races into peace and civilisation. In 1898, the novelist Samuel Odell saw the English-speaking peoples subjugating eastern Europe and Asia by means of aerial bombardment.

None of this was lost on the Wright brothers. When Wilbur Wright was asked, in 1905, what the purpose of his machine might be, he answered simply: "War." As soon as they were confident that the technology worked, the brothers approached the war offices of several nations, hoping to sell their patent to the highest bidder. The US government bought it for $30,000, and started test bombing in 1910. The aeroplane was conceived, designed, tested, developed and sold, in other words, not as a vehicle for tourism, but as an instrument of destruction.

In November 1911, eight years after the first flight, the Italian army carried out the first bombing raid, on a settlement outside Tripoli. Then as now, aerial bombardment was seen as a means of civilising
35 uncooperative peoples. As Sven Lindqvist records in *A History of Bombing*, the imperial powers experimented freely with civilisation from the skies. Just as the Holocaust was prefigured by colonial genocide, so the bombing raids which reduced Guernica, Hamburg, Dresden, Tokyo and parts of London to ash had been
40 rehearsed in north Africa and the Middle East.

As the enemy was reduced to a distant target in an inferior sphere, greater cruelties could be engineered than any effected before. The British knew what they were doing in Germany in World War 2. A directive to Bomber Command in 1942 ordered that the "aiming
45 points" for fire-bombing be "built-up areas, not, for instance, the dockyards or aircraft factories". The Americans knew what they were doing in Japan. Major General Curtis LeMay, who incinerated 100,000 civilians in Tokyo, admitted: "We knew we were going to kill a lot of women and kids when we burned that town. Had to be done." LeMay
50 later became chief of staff of the US airforce and was the man who, in 1964, promised to bomb Vietnam back into the stone age.

I doubt much mention will be made of all this at the centenary celebrations tomorrow. Instead we will be encouraged to concentrate upon the civil applications of this military technology.
55 We will be told how the aeroplane has made the world a smaller place, how it has brought people closer together, fostering understanding and friendship. There is something in this: the people of powerful nations might be reluctant to permit their leaders to destroy the countries they have visited. But commercial flights, like
60 military flights, are an instrument of domination. As tourists, we engage with the people of other nations on our own terms. The world's administrators can flit from place to place enforcing their mandate. The corporate jet-set shrinks the earth to fit its needs. Those with access to the aeroplane control the world.

65   The men who attacked the World Trade Center on September 11
2001 drove one symbol of power into another. The aeroplane, more
precisely than any other technology, represents the global ruling
class. In the past we raised our eyes to the men on horseback; today
we raise our eyes to the heavens.

70   Those hijackers had turned the civilian product of a military
technology back into a military technology, but even when used for
strictly commercial purposes, the airliner remains a weapon of mass
destruction. Last week the World Health Organisation calculated
that climate change is causing 150,000 deaths a year. This figure
75   excludes deaths caused by drought and famine, pests and plant
diseases and conflicts over natural resources, all of which appear to
be exacerbated by global warming. Flying is our most effective
means of wrecking the planet: every passenger on a return journey
from Britain to Florida produces more carbon dioxide than the
80   average motorist does in a year. Every time we fly, we help to kill
someone.

This morning, our government is expected to give a grand 100th
birthday present to the aeroplane. Despite almost 400,000
objections to the expansion of airports in Britain, the transport
85   secretary will announce new runways at Stansted and Birmingham,
and more flights to Heathrow. This, the government hopes, will help
accommodate a near-tripling of the number of journeys into and out
of Britain by 2030. By then the 400,000 won't be the only ones
wishing that Wilbur and Orville (if indeed they were responsible)
90   had stuck to mending bicycles.

Yet just as Alexander the Great worshipped his horse, the US
President and the other enthusiasts for domination will tomorrow, at
10.35am, North Carolina time, bow down before the aeroplane and
worship it. The rest of us should observe 12 seconds of silence, in
95   commemoration of the deeds wrought by those magnificent men in
their killing machines.

Questions

1 Which one of the following statements best sums up the writer's main point?

   A Aeroplanes were developed primarily with warfare in mind.

   B The first successful powered flight was not in America but in New Zealand.

   C Aeroplanes damage the environment and contribute to global warming.

   D No uses of the aeroplane are of benefit to ordinary people.

   E Aeroplanes have been responsible for a great deal of destruction.

2 Which **one** sentence in the passage do you think most clearly expresses the writer's point of view? (Write down the first few words of the sentence or the line references for it.)

3 Which one of the following statements best describes the line of thought in this passage?

   A It is a very balanced discussion of the history and uses of the aeroplane.

   B It is a reasonably balanced discussion of the history and uses of the aeroplane.

   C It is a rather one-sided discussion of the history and uses of the aeroplane.

   D It is a very one-sided discussion of the history and uses of the aeroplane.

Questions

4 Look closely at the final sentence: "The rest of us should observe 12 seconds of silence, in commemoration of the deeds wrought by those magnificent men in their killing machines."

There are several possible reasons for saying this is an effective conclusion to the passage. Here are some possibilities:

(i) it refers to the length of time the Wright brothers were in the air

(ii) it makes the reader think of a "two-minute silence" which is associated with mourning

(iii) it ironically twists the title of a well-known film and song

(iv) it picks up on the earlier reference to "a day of international mourning"

(v) it reminds us that aeroplanes are destructive

(vi) it invites the reader to side with the writer against the people in power

All of these statements are true, but which **three** of them do you think are the strongest reasons for saying that the final sentence is an effective conclusion?

A (ii), (iii) and (vi)

B (i), (v) and (vi)

C (iii), (iv) and (v)

D (i), (ii) and (iv)

Mothers and Fathers

In this passage, from The Independent *newspaper in 2002, Natasha Walter considers the way the media reported the story of the abandonment, by a British couple, of a three-month-old baby in Portugal, and goes on to discuss the importance of both parents when bringing up a child.*

Read the passage straight through to get a general grasp of the writer's attitude to the parents in the news story and her views about child-raising in general. Then answer the questions that follow.

1   Some stories grab the heartstrings of reporters, and a miserable tale of an abandoned baby in Portugal has turned out to be one of them. The details keep shifting, but it goes roughly like this: a British couple were living in Portugal, where they had a baby three months

5   ago. It was reported that they weren't well prepared for the birth, and that the baby had already been put on an "at risk" register in Portugal. A couple of days ago, the baby was left in a pram near Faro airport while the couple caught a flight back to Gatwick. Yesterday, they were questioned by British police.

10   As far as some elements of the British press were concerned, these preliminary facts made it an immediate open season on the woman concerned. "Unforgivable" was the headline in one tabloid newspaper over a picture of the mother trying to hide her face. The story began: "A heartless mum dumped her three-month old baby

15   son on a doorstep in Portugal". "We think she behaved like a bitch," it quoted one friend saying. "Callous bitch," said other friends. The father was hardly mentioned. He was an appendage rather than an actor in the story, and all the blame was hers alone.

      She may be a monster, a callous bitch, and unforgivable. It is a

20   primary offence against decency and love to abandon a child who

needs nothing in the world but your protection, and the sense of outrage that is set off by such an action is understandable. But as well as being an unforgivable bitch, she may also be a confused and desperate woman in need of some support.

25 Some reports said that she didn't mention to anyone, even the child's father, that she was pregnant until she went into labour, that she checked herself out of the maternity hospital against medical advice and then went to work a week after the birth. Was this a woman who was ready to cope with caring for a child in a foreign 30 country?

A tale like this is extreme. It is a tragedy. It is completely atypical of most women's experience of motherhood. But isn't there some more useful response than mere condemnation? Even mothers who never harm their babies and who never feel like walking away from

➤

35 them may still be able to feel some sympathy for women who are unable to rise to the challenge of parenting and who fall into despair.

Motherhood has long been seen as something that comes naturally to women. But as even loving and caring mothers have pointed out,
40 parenting isn't always so straightforward. For most women, a lot of support is necessary if they are to learn to do it well and enjoy it – support that ideally starts in childhood, with the example of their own parents, and goes on through the circles of love and care of their spouse and their friends and their neighbours and their
45 employers. But not everyone lives in that kind of caring, joyful world, and when things are tougher it's not surprising if some women fail to some extent – and that a few fail utterly.

Yet the myth that women should all take to motherhood like ducks to summer ponds still persists, especially in the media, and the
50 assumption that motherhood fits all women like a glove doesn't only make things hard for women and children, it can also make things hard for men. Few women, even today, are ready to say that men can care for children as well as women. Indeed, recent feminist writing has only served to strengthen the mystique of motherhood –
55 they don't think that fathers are worth a dime. So the rash of books about motherhood and domestic work have one striking thing in common: in the homes that we enter through their pages, the men are invisible or useless.

Perhaps that is what men have wanted in the past, to fade into
60 invisibility once their children arrive. But do they still want that? Many men are still eager to rush away from their homes once their children are born, but other men are struggling to become more involved with their children. And I believe that, given the right circumstances, most men would find nurturing and caring for
65 children as natural for them as it is for women.

We have to ask what kind of family life we are building up if men continue to be so marginal to domestic work. Just as it is only honest to admit that many women find motherhood extremely difficult, so it is only honest to say that many men can be fathers who do more than take their kids to the park once a week. In a society where love and time often seem to be in short supply, how can families thrive unless men give more of their love and time to their home lives?

This debate about men in family life needs to grow and gain in power, and it needs to happen among men, as well as among women. It is a debate that has taken a long time to shift, a mountain of inertia that has only been yielding up the odd speck of tumbling gravel. But that doesn't mean we should simply resign ourselves to the status quo. Change is always possible, always imaginable. You can point to small changes in the real world – such as the story earlier this week that a senior civil servant had actually negotiated a contract that included civilised working hours, so that he could spend time with his daughter.

And you can point to shifts in the cultural world. A new book by Ian Sansom provides a great antidote to recent books that place motherhood way above fatherhood. In *The Truth About Babies* he describes the wonder and joy as well as the claustrophobia and frustrations of fatherhood. One of the saddest moments in the book is when he talks about how little historical context he can find for his feelings about being a father. "I can find almost nothing positive in 2000 years of Western culture," he observes.

Who knows, perhaps the next 2000 years will bring a few positive tales about fathering. Men need them, and so do women – and so do children.

Questions

1 Which of the following best sums up the writer's main criticism of the press coverage about the abandoned baby?

   A The press didn't have all the facts.

   B The attack on the mother was very personal.

   C The press merely criticised.

   D The baby's welfare was not discussed.

   E Details of the story were distorted.

   F There was no mention of the father.

2 The writer's attitude to the mother in the story can best be described as:

   A She deserves sympathy.

   B She deserves understanding.

   C She deserves her partner's support.

   D She deserves her friends' support.

3 "… it's not surprising if some women fail to some extent …" (lines 46–47).

What, according to the writer, is the key reason for this failure?

   A Parenting is a complicated process.

   B Parenting needs to be learned over time.

   C Parenting requires support which not everyone has.

   D Parenting is not something all women are suited to.

4 What does the writer see as the most important factor preventing fathers becoming more involved in parenting?

   A the misleading writings of feminists

   B the unsatisfactory reporting in the media

   C the absence of a tradition of fathers enjoying parenthood

   D the lack of interest shown by many men

   E the unhelpful working hours men have to face

Questions

5 "… should take to motherhood like ducks to summer ponds" (lines 48–49).

The more usual turn of phrase would be: "like ducks to water". Why do you think the writer has chosen to alter the well-known phrase in this way?

A to avoid using a cliché

B to create a more vivid simile

C to add a twist to a well-known saying

D to exaggerate the idea of warmth and happiness

Grumpy Old White Men

In this passage, which appeared in The Scotsman *newspaper in November 2004, Joyce McMillan tackles the subject of how well ethnic minorities are accepted in Britain in general and in Scotland in particular. She explores the criticism that "political correctness" is a barrier to good race relations.*

Read the passage straight through, paying particular attention to the writer's attitude to "political correctness", and then answer the questions that follow.

1   It's late November, and time for all the great faiths of the northern hemisphere to turn towards their annual midwinter festivals of light and rebirth: for the Muslim tradition, it's Eid al-Fitr; for the Hindu faith, it's Diwali; in Judaism it's Chanukah; and in the western

5   tradition it's that sparkling combination of Christian and pagan celebration known as Christmas. For a grumpy old man writing in to BBC Radio 4 the other day, however, it's all become a bit too much. He has, he said, been hearing all week, from various "politically correct types" on the BBC, about the celebration of Eid and Diwali,

10   and about the pressure from some quarters to use a neutral term for the midwinter festivals, something like the American "Happy Holidays" rather than saying "Happy Christmas". "Does it ever occur to these people that some of us in Britain might be offended by the celebration of these other faiths?" he asks. "And when," he goes on,

15   "are we going to make it clear that Britain is a Christian country, where other faiths are simply allowed to practise?"

And in some ways, that irritable, wounded response says it all about the strange impasse that race relations in Britain now seem to have reached. On one hand, there is probably wider agreement than ever

20   before that racism itself is an evil that has to be combated; on the other hand, it's difficult to avoid the feeling that this widespread consensus about the evil of racism masks a growing lack of

➤

agreement about what to do about it, and growing anger, in some quarters, against "politically correct" efforts to reverse traditional
25 inequalities.

So what is to be done? Well, in the first place, I think we in Scotland need to acknowledge that we are mere beginners in the art of living in a modern multiracial society. Visible ethnic minorities in Scotland account for less than 2 per cent of the population, compared with
30 almost 10 per cent in the UK as a whole, and 25 per cent in London; and what this means, to put it bluntly, is that most Scots have little experience of living and working with people of different racial backgrounds, and have not got much beyond the point of thinking of black and Asian people in Scotland as "guests" in "our" country –
35 although it only takes a moment to imagine how patronising and inadequate that attitude must seem, for example, to young Scots Asians born here.

➣

Then secondly, we all need to stop bristling, sulking, and taking refuge in petulance every time anyone accuses us of racism. Fear of the
40 unfamiliar and the unknown is a natural human response; racism is an aspect of that response, and we all experience it. The question is whether we allow that fear to override the civilised civic impulse to believe the best of all our fellow-citizens, to approach them as equals, and to include them in every aspect of our society; or whether we seek
45 to recognise our fear, put it to one side, and ensure that the positive civic impulse triumphs. And if it is "politically correct" to expect those in our society to make that effort towards self-awareness, then political correctness is clearly a damned good thing – or at any rate, vastly preferable to the huffy and defensive rejection of cultural
50 change in all its forms that seems to be the main alternative on offer.

What is true, though, is that it is difficult for people to accept change or to engage in constructive self-criticism when they feel profoundly threatened; and this is where the wounded feelings of the writer to the BBC come into play. Of course, the celebration of
55 Eid and Diwali in Britain presents no real threat to Christmas, or to Christianity. But those things are threatened, nonetheless, by the growing secularism of a society in which most children no longer have any experience of worship, Christian or otherwise; in which the old Bible stories that used to form the bedrock of our culture go
60 increasingly untold; and in which the feast that is supposed to mark the birth of the founder of Christianity has become, for millions, little more than a gross materialistic blowout.

Add that recognition of a declining Christian tradition to the raging insecurities caused by a generation of breakneck economic and
65 social change – not least in our most intimate family relationships – and you begin to understand the cocktail of miseries that makes some traditionally-minded people turn against one of the most obvious physical signs of change in our society, and start blaming Britain's increasingly confident ethnic minorities for everything from
70 rising crime rates to declining church attendance.

➤

But in truth, people who indulge in that knee-jerk hostility to ethnic minorities, and to official efforts to include these minorities more fully in our society, are making a mistake that is as foolish as it is indefensible. For in any battle between spirituality and materialism,
75 between ignorant contempt for the past and decent respect for it, between family or community values and rampant selfish individualism, the fact is that Britain's ethnic minorities are more likely to side with moral traditionalists, rather than against them.

And the sooner Britain's grumpy old white men get out of their
80 cultural ghettos and start finding out just how true that is, the sooner we can perhaps stop the unproductive whining about "political correctness" that has become a universal excuse for complacency and inaction on equality issues among Britain's conservative middle classes.

Questions

1 Which one of the following statements best sums up the writer's main point in this passage?

 A Political correctness is destroying race relations in this country.

 B Political correctness is irritating to some people but it promotes proper attitudes.

 C Political correctness is preventing different groups from getting on with each other.

 D Political correctness is preferable to racist attitudes.

 E Political correctness is a damned good thing.

2 Read lines 38–50 again carefully, and then decide which of the following best describes the writer's attitude to racism:

 A It is understandable but wrong.

 B It is understandable and shouldn't be criticised.

 C It is increasing at an alarming rate.

 D It is declining thanks to political correctness.

 E It is evil and should be stamped out.

 F It is evil but can never be stamped out.

3 Which of the following statements best describes the writer's attitude to the man who wrote in to the BBC?

 A He is quite correctly standing up for what he believes in.

 B He is a dangerous racist.

 C He is a stupid old fool.

 D He is unaware of what ethnic minorities actually believe.

 E He is wrong about the threat to Christianity.

A Parable for our Times

On 30th January 2007, it was announced that the city of Manchester had been chosen ahead of London and Blackpool as the site of Britain's first "supercasino". The next day, in The Times *newspaper, writer and journalist Magnus Linklater offered his thoughts on the decision.*

Read the passage straight through in order to get a general grasp of Linklater's response to the decision and his attitude to gambling in general. (Note: "Moss Side" (line 26) and "Alexandra Park" (line 32) are districts in Manchester.) Then answer the questions that follow.

1   It is a parable for our times that Manchester is celebrating today because it has successfully bid to be the gambling capital of Britain. The place where cotton once was king, the hub of the industrial revolution, the home of Victorian social reformers such as Cobden,
5   Bright and Owen who championed the workers, has become … the city of bling. What were the odds? Seven to one against, evens or just pile all the money on red and hope for the best?

These days, it seems, bringing in the high rollers, the poker dudes and those inert rows of zombies who spend their days pulling the
10   levers on fruit machines becomes every bit as important as attracting a multimillion-pound semiconductor plant or going for the Commonwealth Games. The bidding process sounds much the same – emphasise phrases like "world-class venue", "state-of-the-art transport system", "areas of deprivation" and, of course,
15   "regeneration" and it all begins to come together. But, when the chips are down, is that regeneration – or degeneration?

There are two ways to view this government-sponsored gambling fever. One is to bemoan the dumbing down of our national life and

➤

somehow hope that it will all go away; or to find out whether
20 Manchester can strike a balance between the tourist expansion that
its new supercasino is said to offer, and the sleazy subculture and
gambling addiction that could grow up around it. It is a tough call.

For more than a generation, Manchester has been grappling with
gangs, gun crime and drugs. It is not so long ago that shootings were
25 almost routine in the city's bleaker housing estates. But Manchester
has finally begun to gain the upper hand. Moss Side, once a byword
for violence, has turned the corner, taken down the worst of its
slums and rebuilt its police and community relations to such an
extent that a place that was once so violent that taxi drivers simply
30 would not go there now has a housing waiting list.

Race relations, which caused riots on the streets 25 years ago, have
markedly improved. Alexandra Park, the so-called "drug-dealing

supermarket for North West England", now has falling rates of crime; drug use is markedly down.

35   To inject a Las Vegas-style supercasino into this fragile recovery programme might seem, at first sight, like madness. On the east side of Manchester, a 5,000 sq metre complex is to be built, housing more than 1,200 jackpot gaming machines, with unlimited stakes. In a relatively deprived area of town, where gambling is often seen as

40   the only way out of poverty, the temptations of round-the-clock blackjack, poker or roulette may prove irresistible. We already have a national addiction to gambling, with poker sites the fastest-growing on the web. A supercasino, along with the chain of smaller-sized gambling outlets planned across Britain, could simply feed this

45   habit.

There is, however, more force to the argument made by the Government that licensing approved casinos is a way of introducing regulations to curb the excesses of gambling rather than leaving them to the uncontrolled regime of the internet or the criminal

50   underworld.

You cannot ignore a social revolution, however much you might deplore it, and what has happened over the past decade is that the rarefied world of high-class betting, once the preserve of exclusive London clubs such as Aspinalls, or indulged by the international jet-

55   set in resorts such as Monte Carlo, has been opened up to a wider clientele. Gambling has become the leisure activity of the masses. Instead of patronising their local betting shop, they have gone online in their millions to play poker with the best of them. It is pure snobbery to argue that they should go back to the smoky retreats of

60   their local bookies, on the condescending grounds that they cannot be trusted with the challenges of "proper" gambling.

It is therefore up to any city entrusted with a supercasino to ensure that gambling is well run, sensibly managed and properly regulated.

➤

I would trust Manchester to do that better than the other cities that
65 competed with it and lost. The prospect of Blackpool, with its
tawdry seaside attractions, or the Millennium Dome in London, with
its dubious American backer and unhealthy political connections,
taking on a project so complex and so fraught would not have
inspired great confidence.

70 Manchester has already shown that it can manage big events, can
deliver projects on time and, more to the point, has the kind of
leadership that shows it has a clear idea of how and where it wants
to develop its city. It has recovered from two great disasters – the
death of its great industries, which left a legacy of slums and
75 unemployment, and the 1996 IRA bomb, which destroyed many of
the new buildings in its city centre. This recovery has put the city
back on the map as the undisputed capital of the North West.

The last thing it will want to do is put all that at risk by transforming
itself into a downmarket gaming resort blighted by sleaze, vulgarity
80 and crime. If its stern, nonconformist past means anything,
Manchester will ensure that the leisure centre it plans, the jobs it
will spawn and the new climate it will create in the city do not bring
with them the virus of corruption, and that it controls rather than
fosters the gambling addiction that ruins people's lives.

85 Far be it from me to inject a hedonistic note into the argument, but
for most of those who do it, gambling is, after all, quite good fun.

Questions

I The writer says in lines 17–18: "There are two ways to view this government-sponsored gambling fever."

(a) In light of your reading of the whole passage, which of the two ways do you think the writer favours?

A "… bemoan the dumbing down of our national life and somehow hope that it will all go away …" (lines 18–19)

B "… find out whether Manchester can strike a balance between the tourist expansion that its new supercasino is said to offer, and the sleazy subculture and gambling addiction that could grow up around it …" (lines 19–22)

(b) Quote the clearest evidence you can find in the whole passage to support your answer.

2 The writer mentions several features of Manchester's past and present:

(i) the way its has dealt with "gangs, gun crime and drugs" (line 24)

(ii) the improvement in race relations (lines 31–32)

(iii) its "leadership" (lines 71–73)

(iv) its recovery from "two great disasters" (lines 73–77)

(v) "its stern, nonconformist past" (line 80)

Which two of these features seem to be most important in making the writer "trust Manchester to do better than the other cities" (line 64)?

A (ii) and (iii)

B (i) and (iv)

C (iii) and (v)

D (ii) and (iv)

E (i) and (v)

Questions

3 (a) What is the "social revolution" to which the writer refers in line 51?

    A the idea that gambling is seen as a way out of poverty

    B the arrival of internet gambling

    C the decline of local betting shops

    D it is now not just rich people who gamble for pleasure

    E the growth of a national addiction to gambling

(b) What appears to be the writer's attitude to the "social revolution"?

    A He approves of it.

    B He disapproves of it.

    C He passes no judgement.

The Trial of Lady Chatterley

The passage which follows is from The Swinging Sixties *by Brian Masters, published in 1985. The book explores a number of the social, political and artistic changes in Britain during the 1960s. In this extract, the author describes an important event in 1960 when a publisher was taken to court to prevent its publishing a novel which was alleged to be obscene.*

Read the passage straight through in order to get a general grasp of the background to the trial, of the trial itself, and of Masters' consideration of its impact. Then answer the questions that follow.

1   In 1955 a bookseller was sentenced by a local magistrate in Hornsey,
    north London, to two months' imprisonment for "handling" a novel
    by D. H. Lawrence, *Lady Chatterley's Lover*. The fact that this was
    a major, if flawed, novel by one of the twentieth century's finest
5   writers was not held to be the point; it was indecent and obscene
    because it described on several occasions sexual congress between
    Lady Chatterley and her gardener, Mellors, and used a fair smattering
    of "four-letter words" to describe some of the activities. For this
    reason, Lawrence's novel had been banned for thirty years - you
10 could buy it in Paris and, if you dared, smuggle it through Her
    Majesty's Customs into Britain, but the penalties were high.

    The 1959 Obscene Publications Act was an attempt to distinguish
    between the frankly erotic and the genuinely artistic, between
    books which have a tendency "to deprave and corrupt" and those
15 which do not. Unfortunately, the Act was badly drafted in a number
    of ways. The distinctions were not clear, the vocabulary susceptible
    to too many interpretations. It was left open to debate how one
    person might be depraved and corrupted by a book and another not,

➤

how the resulting depravity might be measured or proven, or what,
20 in the end, obscenity actually meant. All this gave the Act a club-foot
over which it was to stumble so many times in the ensuing years that
the battle between censors and liberationists in Britain became a
long-running and highly enjoyable comedy.

The first and most famous of these cases was the trial of *Lady*
25 *Chatterley's Lover*, which had circulated surreptitiously for a long
time in foreign editions, and latterly in an American edition. D. H.
Lawrence was highly respected in literary circles (it seems
superfluous, even insulting, to write this now, but it was not by any
means so in 1960) and his work was studied at universities. Yet no
30 course on Lawrence which required consideration of *Lady*
Chatterley's Lover could offer copies of the book to students, as
none legally existed. The situation was patently ridiculous, and
someone sooner or later would have to do something about it.

➢

The most famous paperback publishing house in the English-
35 speaking world, Penguin Books, had an illustrious record of making
the great classics of literature available in cheap editions. 1960
would mark their twenty-fifth anniversary and, coincidentally, the
thirtieth anniversary of the death of D. H. Lawrence. To celebrate
the double event, they announced in January 1960 plans to publish
40 eight of Lawrence's books including *Lady Chatterley's Lover*.
Penguin had a shrewd idea that they would not only make
publishing history but a pretty penny as well, and printed an
advance of 200,000 copies. Then they tactfully sent a dozen copies
to the Director of Public Prosecutions (DPP) as a statement of intent,
45 whereupon the DPP immediately declared he would prosecute
under the Obscene Publications Act. Penguin kept their stocks
closely locked up pending proceedings, and prepared to do battle.

The saga may have been short-lived had it not been for the chance
which placed upon the scene, as prosecuting counsel, Mr Mervyn
50 Griffith-Jones, a man of extraordinary obtuseness and antediluvian
attitudes. He manifestly believed Lawrence's book to be lewd and
worthless, and that it was his mission to stem a tide of wickedness
and reconfirm the proper values of literature. His only witness
would be the book itself, since its degradation and iniquity must be
55 obvious to anyone who had the misfortune to read it.

The trial took place in November 1960, lasted six days and aroused
intense public interest. Its most celebrated moment occurred within
the first hour, when Griffith-Jones in his opening address to the jury
said:

60 "You may think that one of the ways in which you can read this
book, and test it from the most liberal outlook, is to ask yourselves
the question, when you have read it through, would you approve of
your young sons, young daughters – because girls can read as well as
boys – reading this book. Is it a book that you would have lying
65 around in your house? Is it a book that you would wish your wife or
your servants to read?"

➤

Not surprisingly, there was a rumble of laughter in the court.

Unchastened, Griffith-Jones went on to list the exact number of times certain offensive words occurred in the text. He did not
70 disclose whether he had counted them himself. So confident was he in the purity of his case that he told the amazed courtroom that he did not intend to call any witnesses at all. (It was only much later that news leaked out that he had been unable to find a single professor or author willing to testify against the book.)

75 Defence counsel on the other hand produced authors, clerics, dons, journalists, who paraded into the witness box to sing the praises of D. H. Lawrence so fulsomely that it became embarrassing. This was all too much for Mr Griffith-Jones, who, it was becoming increasingly clear, felt the prosecution should really be directed at Lady
80 Chatterley for allowing herself to be possessed by someone other than her husband. Not only that, but her gardener to boot! This second theme, that such goings-on should not be admitted between people of different classes, constantly underlay his questioning.

The jury found Penguin Books not guilty. Two million copies were
85 then sold within twelve months, and nearly seven million have been sold to date.

The trial of *Lady Chatterley's Lover* (and indeed of Lady Chatterley) was an important event, and a signal pointing towards the tone of the decade to come. Within a very short time it would
90 seem unthinkable that the British had tolerated censorship well into the second half of the twentieth century, or had pilloried a citizen of whom they should have been proud. It would of course be misleading to suggest that the Sixties forever stilled the voices of those who would tell us what we can and cannot read. They are still
95 about. What it did do was to give those voices a microphone, so that their rhetoric could be heard and exposed, subdued and ultimately ignored.

Questions

1 When he explains the background to the trial, the writer mixes fact with personal comment. On which of the following does he express an opinion? Refer to statements (i) to (v) below.

(i) the quality of the novel *Lady Chatterley's Lover*

(ii) the fact that the book was banned

(iii) the fact that it couldn't be studied at University

(iv) the Obscene Publications Act of 1959

(v) Penguin Books' motives in planning to publish the book

A (i), (ii) and (iii) only

B (i), (ii), (iv) and (v) only

C (ii), (iii), (iv) and (v) only

D (iii), (iv) and (v) only

E all of them

2 Look at Masters' account of the trial (lines 48–83).

(a) Which of the following gives the main reason (according to the writer) for the verdict:

    A The defence counsel was very effective.

    B The prosecuting counsel had such old-fashioned ideas.

    C The prosecuting counsel was so stupid.

    D Nobody would testify against the novel.

    E Lots of people were willing to praise the book.

(b) Referring in detail to lines 60–66, explain as clearly as you can why "there was a rumble of laughter in the court" (line 67).

Questions

3   Select the most accurate completion to the following sentence:

According to the writer's conclusion, the trial of *Lady Chatterley's Lover* . . .

A   . . .brought censorship in Britain to an end.

B   . . .went a long way to making censorship in Britain unacceptable.

C   . . .gave an indication of what the Sixties would be like.

D   . . .restored the reputation of D. H. Lawrence.

E   . . .had little or no effect on censorship in Britain.

The Blue Rigi

Writing in The Times *in January 2007, Ben Macintyre describes the campaign to raise money so that a famous painting by the English watercolourist J. M. W. Turner (1775–1851) can be kept in Britain. He goes on to explore the importance of art to a nation's sense of identity.*

Note: the "Ruskin" referred to in lines 25 and 83 was a writer, poet and artist, but was best known as an art critic; "the looters on Branscombe beach" (lines 31–32) refers to the large numbers of people who took away goods washed up on a Devonshire beach from the wrecked container ship "Napoli"; the "Mr Brown" referred to in lines 73 and 85 was, at the time of writing, Chancellor of the Exchequer (in charge of the country's money) and was hoping to become Prime Minister.

Read the passage straight through to get a general grasp of why Macintyre thinks The Blue Rigi in particular and art in general are important. Then answer the questions that follow.

1 I bought a painting by Turner yesterday. Not any old Turner, mind you, but The Blue Rigi, probably his finest watercolour, that luminously beautiful vision of the glimmering dawn on Rigi mountain across Lake Lucerne.

5 OK, I didn't buy the whole picture. I paid for exactly one pixel's worth online, the equivalent of a single Turner brushstroke, and it cost me £5.

My fiver represents one nine-hundred-and-ninety-thousandth of the sum that will be needed to keep The Blue Rigi in Britain. Last year
10 the painting was purchased by a private foreign buyer, thought to be American, for £5.8 million. The Culture Ministry placed a temporary export bar on the Turner, and now the Art Fund charity, the

National Heritage Memorial Fund and the public have until March 20 to raise enough cash to match the sale price.

15   Any member of the public can now click on a tiny fraction of the painting, and pay a tiny fraction of what is needed to keep it here. As a way to raise money for preserving British art in Britain, this seems brilliantly simple, highly inventive – and rather desperate. In most countries a supreme national artefact like this would never
20   even go on sale; in Britain we must scrabble to hold on to it, one pixel at a time.

Why is The Blue Rigi worth the effort and expense? First, some superlatives. It is the most expensive British watercolour ever sold, representing the pinnacle of achievement by a genius who
25   revolutionised the art. Ruskin called The Blue Rigi and its two sister

paintings of the same scene as "the noblest landscapes ever conceived by human intellect".

The Blue Rigi is exquisitely lovely, a foreign scene but uniquely British. Painted in 1842, when Turner was approaching his mellow
30 seventies, it stands in contrast to the melodrama of his earlier work, a vision of tranquil reflection like no other. If the scenes of the looters on Branscombe beach and the screaming nonentities on Celebrity Big Brother appal you, go and see The Blue Rigi for a contrasting British sensibility. I defy anyone to look at this painting
35 and not feel a certain serenity, a flicker of pride.

The struggle to pay for The Blue Rigi is part of a wider crisis. With auction prices spiralling upwards and museum acquisition budgets dwindling, important cultural artefacts are steadily disappearing. Simply put, our museums cannot outbid the Russian oligarchs, the
40 technology billionaires and the American megamuseums.

For every artwork saved for the nation amid great fanfare, dozens of other beautiful and rare treasures slip quietly away. In 2005 nine objects of vital artistic importance worth £5.6 million were saved after export bans; but another 16 objects, worth £41 million, could
45 not be saved. We are rapidly approaching the situation of an aristocrat flogging off heirlooms. First of all the Georgian silver goes. And then all that nice furniture that used to be in the drawing room. Then the Canalettos.

Of course there will always be a conflict between the demands of
50 commerce and those of culture. The free market in art cannot be prevented from operating like any another, and nor should it, but there are numerous (though expensive) ways to tip the balance in favour of our own museums.

For a start, any individual donating art to the nation should receive
55 at least some income tax relief. In France 90 per cent relief is

➤

available, and in the US 100 per cent; an improved tax break would encourage greater artistic philanthropy in this country.

When an object of supreme cultural importance is about to go on the market, British museums should be given a head start in the sales
60 process, long before the frenzy of the auction room takes over. They should also be allowed a longer period to raise money when a temporary export ban has been granted. At the same time, it seems bizarre that under current rules only objects more than 50 years old may be subject to an export ban: that leaves a wealth of important
65 and valuable modern work by the likes of Hockney and Freud open to immediate foreign sale.

Campaigners this week called for the Government to set up a £1 billion emergency fund to ensure that the 25 most important artworks in private hands can be bought by the nation rather than
70 sold abroad. It has been calculated that if even half that sum had been set aside, then every export crisis of the last decade could have been solved.

Mr Brown is anxious to find and reassert a sense of Britishness. One of the most emphatic ways to do so would be to spend Government
75 money ensuring that the best examples of British art, and art in Britain, remain here. Part of being British is a collective appreciation of the treasures we have created and collected. No "Institute of Britishness" could define what that word means better than a subtle Turner landscape. Protecting the national artistic heritage can only
80 be done with a substantial financial commitment from the Government: every £5 pixel helps, but this is a crisis requiring broad brush strokes, not pointillism.

Ruskin wrote of the Rigi series: "Turner had never made any drawings like these before, and never made any like them again. He
85 is not showing his hand in these, but his heart." If Mr Brown wants to show us his British heart, he must put his hand in his pocket.

Questions

1   Why, according to the writer, is art such as The Blue Rigi important?

  A It is beautiful to look at.

  B It is part of our national identity.

  C It is worth huge amounts of money.

  D It shows what British artists can achieve.

2   Why, according to the writer, is it difficult to keep artworks such as The Blue Rigi in Britain?

  A People in other countries have much more money.

  B British people do not recognise the quality of the works.

  C British people do not realise the importance of the works.

  D The British government is not prepared to spend enough money.

3   In lines 54–72 the writer refers to five practical suggestions which he thinks would make it easier for artworks like The Blue Rigi to be kept in Britain. From your understanding of the writer's beliefs from the passage as a whole, rank these in order to show what he thinks is the most important step to take. (Put the "most important" first.)

  A Give tax relief to those who donate art to the nation.

  B British museums should be allowed to show an interest early in the sale.

  C British museums should be allowed longer to raise the money.

  D Art less than 50 years old should be protected.

  E The Government should set up an emergency fund.

Questions

4 In the opening three paragraphs (lines 1–14) the writer aims for a very conversational, informal style of writing – combined with moments of very rich description.

(a) Which **three** of the following six quotations do you think make the most effective contribution to establishing the conversational, informal style of writing?

    A "I bought a painting by Turner yesterday."

    B "Not any old Turner, mind you ..."

    C "OK ..."

    D "... it cost me £5"

    E "My fiver ..."

    F "... raise enough cash ..."

(b) Which **one** of the following do you think makes the most effective contribution to the very rich description?

    A "... his finest watercolour ..."

    B "... luminously ..."

    C "... beautiful vision ..."

    D "... glimmering dawn ..."

5 In lines 15–21, the writer compares Britain unfavourably with "most countries". Which **two** of the following best convey the writer's contempt for the British approach?

    (i) "... a tiny fraction ..."

    (ii) "... rather desperate ..."

    (iii) "... scrabble ..."

    (iv) "... one pixel at a time"

    A (i) and (ii)

    B (ii) and (iii)

    C (iii) and (iv)

    D (i) and (iii)

Passage Nineteen

The Explosive Device

The passage below is an extract from the book The Printed Word *by Christopher Small, published in 1982. In a chapter entitled "The Explosive Device", Small considers the changes brought about by the invention of printing, and considers the way it changed the transmission of ideas.*

Read the passage straight through to get a general grasp of the writer's argument about the benefits of printing. Then answer the questions that follow.

1 The invention of printing is, obviously, a crucial event in modern history: "modern times", that vaguely-defined period, can be said to have begun with it. The five centuries since Gutenberg set up his press in Mainz have been shaped in profound and varied ways by the device,
5 in essence extremely simple, of reproducing a text, in identical and virtually unlimited number, by means of movable type; the same device, modified and extended, has been a potent instrument in spreading European power and influence throughout the world.

Whether Gutenberg or another produced the first European book
10 printed by movable type is disputed and not perhaps very important. What is certain is that printing, like certain other technological innovations – the making and use of gunpowder, for example – was a rapid and spectacular success. Half a century after the appearance of Gutenberg's 42-line Latin Bible, there were
15 hundreds of printing-shops in cities all over the continent. Thousands of books, tens of thousands and even, according to one calculation, millions of copies, were already being turned out; however primitive the means, compared with later refinements, the possibility of mass production was present from the beginning. This
20 in itself gave the printed word what may be thought its most significant characteristic: the triumph of mere number, or multiplication, over any restriction that might be placed on it.

➤

In contests between authority anxious to control opinion and authors trying to disseminate heretical or unorthodox notions the printing press gave dissidence a new and enormous advantage – something which was to remain an attribute of words in print for a long time, if not quite to this day.

The very term "publisher", in the sense of someone making writings available to the public at large, only begins to be used at this time; and the whole idea of the book as communication and store of thought and information began rapidly to alter. When books were reproduced only in manuscript and the number of copies was strictly limited, the potential readership was so to speak "linear": a book might have an indefinitely extended succession of readers through time (and books were made, as material objects, to last) but only as handed on from one person to another.

Not only and obviously did this make it unlikely that literacy should be other than a specialised skill, but it strongly tended to make books the transmitters of tradition rather than the means of
40 disseminating novelty. Printed books, on the other hand, could be and were spread abroad "laterally", to many readers at once, with quite different effects: the proliferation of presses and bookseller-publishers from northern Europe to Spain had consequences quite without precedent, ensuring a wider diffusion of ideas than
45 Europeans had ever been able to conceive as possible.

The dissemination, or sowing, of ideas was not of course impossible before the advent of print. It was carried out, slowly, by writing, and rapidly by speech. In many ways probably "word of mouth" was – and is – the most rapid and economical means of making something
50 widely known; it is notorious that certain kinds of news especially, the kind known as rumour, spreads faster by mouth to ear than anything that has to be read.

Books, however, or more simply writing, have always had important advantages as a means of communication. Books are accurate – that
55 is to say, they are not subject to unavoidable modification which oral information suffers in passing from hearer to hearer. They constitute a permanent record which can be checked: what a man merely says, even with oaths, he can later deny, but what he has set down is there in evidence. Books have been able to overcome both space
60 and time. They can be sent where their authors cannot go; they can outlast a man's personal life, and transmit his thoughts to future generations, in theory at least, without limit. Because they can be read over and over, and compared with one another, they are far more suitable than speech for conveying complex ideas.

65 The transmission in former times of the equivalent of whole volumes of information and tradition, all by word of mouth, is something we today can barely understand. But the important point to note is the selectiveness of verbal teaching, by which knowledge

➢

is transmitted only to suitable persons, a chosen few; while writing,
70 an inanimate go-between, cannot control its readers in any way. It is
a problem which has troubled men, especially those of an
authoritarian cast of mind, ever since books were around and liable
to fall into the hands of "the wrong sort" of reader.

The invention of printing enormously exacerbated the problem.
75 Originally described simply as mechanical handwriting, it hugely
and precipitately enhanced the powers of written communication.
The transformation from "linear" to "lateral" was more than mere
multiplication, though it was multiplication that brought it about:
almost at once the effect of indiscriminate distribution, began to
80 show as never before.

Books, with their power to outreach and outlast the frailties of
mortal memory, were powerful transmitters and sustainers of
tradition, and had until the invention of printing operated in the
main within a minority only; there was an "educated culture"
85 nourished by reading and writing, and there was a "popular" or
illiterate culture transmitted by word of mouth. Print began at once
to demolish the distinction; books suddenly took on the possibility
of becoming a means, if not at once the chief means, of
disseminating knowledge and ideas to all and sundry. The very
90 possibility helped to create the feeling that all and sundry not only
might but ought to have the chance to receive them.

Questions

1   Which one of the following benefits of printing does the writer consider the most important?

  A It allowed ideas to be transmitted at great speed.

  B It allowed ideas to be transmitted without being controlled.

  C It allowed ideas to be transmitted in multiple copies.

  D It allowed ideas to be transmitted without being distorted.

  E It allowed ideas to be transmitted to huge numbers of people.

  F It allowed ideas to be transmitted after the death of the writer.

2   Why do you think the writer chose to call the chapter from which this extract is taken "The Explosive Device"?

  A because printing brought about extremely powerful changes

  B because he thinks that printing had a potentially dangerous effect

  C because he compares printing at one point to the invention of gunpowder

  D because he considers that printing destroyed other means of communication

  E because printing had an effect which could not be reversed

The Casino Culture

In January 2007, it was announced that Britain's first "supercasino" would be built in Manchester. Writing in The Telegraph *newspaper soon after the announcement, the political commentator Simon Heffer discusses the subject of gambling and the extent to which it should be regulated.*

Read the passage straight through in order to get a general grasp of Heffer's attitude to gambling and whether it should be regulated by the Government. Then answer the questions that follow.

1   I wonder whether it ever occurs to gamblers why it is that we have such a successful bookmaking industry in this country? It is because the one thing you can bet on – I speak metaphorically, of course – is that the bookmaker always wins. Yet, despite this proof of how the
5   odds are rigorously stacked against them, punters still punt.

  Human nature, though, is a bizarre thing. Some people smoke packets of cigarettes a day, even though a visit to any terminal ward will show them the likely, and ghastly, results of the habit. Others will be unable to resist that last whisky before getting behind the
10   wheel of a car, even though they know that policemen with breathalysers, or, worse, harmless pedestrians, may strew their road home. And the announcement of our first "super-casino", and 16 other smaller establishments, widens the potential for self-destruction. Some people will punt that last hundred or thousand,
15   knowing their family will go without if they lose, or even that they might finally be driven under financially.

  Given that society and the law, quite correctly, do not rule out an element of risk in all our lives, it might be hard to see why this matters. It is not only that all sorts of other harms remain available

➤

20   for us to inflict on ourselves: it is that, if we wish to gamble now, and indeed lose epic amounts of money in the process, we can do so. We cannot merely walk into a branch of a bookmaker and put piles of money on a horse or a football match: we can do it over the telephone or, at any hour of the day or night, lose our shirts on the

25   internet. Some websites are regulated, with limits of how often the punter can gamble and how much he can lose in a session: others are not. There was the story last year about a teenager who, using his father's credit card, lost £30,000 in an evening on an unregulated site.

30   It is not my instinctively old-fashioned attitude to life that causes me to feel such despair at the creation of a casino culture in Britain. It is that I feel that, while gambling will always continue just as smoking and drinking to excess will, it is no place of the Government to facilitate it. Indeed, the Government should look very hard at the

➤

35   gambling that already exists, and ask whether what we have is regulated enough.

Gambling has, down the centuries, caused much harmless pleasure. It has also caused enormous human misery. Worse even than that, perhaps, is the way it demoralises society, by enabling the severance
40   of the link between effort and reward. There will be casualties of more gambling, and somebody will have to pay to pick up the pieces. Given our obsession with welfare, it will not inevitably be the individuals concerned. And this is a way of life that the Government now proposes to make much easier, and to encourage
45   as quite morally acceptable.

Why has the Government done this? Quite simply, because it sees another means - following the success of the National Lottery - of imposing a tax on stupidity, and relieving the public of its money. The siting of the super-casino in Manchester is fabulously cynical:
50   for it is positioned near a huge centre of population, and close to the wealthiest area of the country outside the South East, so guarantees three oranges on the Treasury's fruit machine every day. This is not about "regeneration" (do me a favour) or about "regulating gambling" (ditto), this is about finding a new revenue stream -
55   whatever the moral implications or the human cost.

For many people today, in an age when gambling has reached proportions unimaginable 40 years ago and when high-stakes gambling is no longer the province of the very rich, casinos for the masses is a preventable evil. It is no figment of the imagination that
60   gambling addiction, divorce, bankruptcy, poverty and crime can all stem from this jolly tax-raising pastime. Oh, I know people must be allowed to take risks - and I am more than happy for them to do so, provided the only casualties if things go wrong are themselves. But with gambling, that is rarely going to be the case. Spouses suffer.
65   Children suffer. In the case of the teenager and the credit card, parents suffered. And, since the workhouse has been abolished, the

➤

taxpayer suffers, because the welfare state will inevitably step in and provide a safety net.

70 I am not going to get in to all the add-on depravities that we are told go with American casinos in places like Las Vegas and Atlantic City – such as drugs and prostitution – because for the moment they are unquantifiable. Would anyone, though, bet that they will not soon emerge as part of the culture here, as they have elsewhere? The addictive and amoral climate that surrounds American casinos 75 certainly encourages them. Why should that not be the case here?

As a libertarian, I am not opposed to gambling. All I ask is that the Government would be more honest about the social (as opposed to personal) risks associated with the gambling culture among lower- and middle-income people, and to seek to provide against that 80 preventable evil by giving this vice no further encouragement.

After all: can somebody explain to me the difference between legalising casinos, because of the huge rake-off the Government can take in taxation and, say, legalising brothels? Lots of people are happy to engage in both of these activities. The revenue possibilities 85 from legalising brothels are potentially enormous. They wouldn't actually regenerate anywhere, and there would be severe social consequences, but we appear to be able to take such things on the chin when it comes to casinos, so why not legalise prostitutes while we're at it?

Questions

1   According to the writer, what is the main reason for the Government's support for the development of new casinos?

   A   Gambling does no more harm than alcohol or tobacco.

   B   The areas where casinos are sited will benefit.

   C   A lot of money will be raised in taxation.

   D   It will make the Government popular with the voters.

   E   The Government will be able to control the amount of gambling.

2   Which one of the following states the writer's main objection to the Government's encouragement of gambling?

   A   Gambling causes social problems which affect everyone.

   B   Gambling attracts criminal elements such as drugs and prostitution.

   C   Gambling allows people to think you can be rich without working.

   D   Gambling encourages people to take risks.

3   The writer describes himself as a "libertarian" (line 76). From your reading of the whole passage, which one of the following do you think best describes what this means:

   A   a person who is in favour of as little Government intervention as possible

   B   a person who thinks gambling is a harmless activity

   C   a person who thinks that social problems require everyone's attention

   D   a person who thinks that Government has a large part to play in people's lives

   E   a person who believes people should be allowed to do whatever they want

4   In the final paragraph the writer suggests the legalisation of brothels. What reason does he give for this?

   A   It would make lots of money for the Government.

   B   It would be logical since gambling is legal.

   C   It would allow people to do something they enjoyed.

   D   It would reduce the dangers associated with prostitution.